Before You Call I Will Answer

Before You Call I Will Answer

David A. Redding

Guideposts

CARMEL • NEW YORK 10512

Acknowledgment is made for permission to use the following copyrighted material:

Psalm by Aleksandr Solzhenitsyn from A Chronicle of Current Events, Number 50, 1979 (English translation © Amnesty International).

Prayer by Aleksandr Solzhenitsyn, copyright David A. Redding.

Prayers on pp. 58 and 59 from The Prayers I Love; selected by David A. Redding, calligraphy by Alice Girand: 1978. Used by permission of the publisher, Strawberry Hill Press.

Chapter 4, which is taken from JESUS MAKES ME LAUGH by David A. Redding. Copyright © 1977 by the Zondervan Corporation. Used by permission.

Chapter 13, which originally appeared in Life magazine, April 18, 1960.

Chapters 7 and 8, which are from Psalms of David by David A. Redding, Fleming H. Revell Company, copyright © 1963.

Excerpt from pages 109–115, Volume I from Mark Twain's Autobiography, with an Introduction by Albert Bigelow Paine. Copyright 1924 by Clara Gabrilowitsch. Copyright renewed, 1952, by Clara Clemens Samossoud. Reprinted by permission of Harper & Row, Publishers, Inc.

"Daylight," by John Russell (Hondo) Crouch used by permission of Grape Creek Music.

Library of Congress Cataloging in Publication Data

Redding, David A.
Before you call, I will answer.

1. Prayer 2. Prayers. I. Title
BV210.2.R33 1985   248.3'2   84-22845
ISBN 0-8007-1411-3

TO

the Glory of God and with joy on the safe
arrival of my twin grandchildren,
Alexei and Katrina
February 25, 1984

Contents

Acknowledgments

Doris Woods Cary
Elizabeth Walter Dixon
Velma Young Pierce
Dorothy McCleery Redding

Before they call, I will answer;
and while they are yet speaking,
I will hear.

Isaiah 65:24

I'M JUST A PRAYER AWAY

O God
How poor I am
How rich if I could
Still have prayer

O God how low I am
My mortal flight
Is on one floor

But I am tired of sitting on
These chairs. Homesick
For that upper room

It makes me think of
Those old altar stairs
And wonder
If they would still
Hold my weight

There was a door up there
He used to keep unlocked
The latch was low,
And I could always open it
If I got down
Upon my knees

Preface

And He taught them "... always to pray and not lose heart" (Luke 18:1 RSV). He did? They taught us never to pray. It was illegal during school, and after school it was a laugh. A recent film has a castaway straining for words at a funeral: "Our Father Who art in heaven ... with liberty and justice for all." Prayer has turned into a problem. They have taken it to court.

Did prayer flop in church—dry up in long faces and disappear into sweet nothings? Mark Twain's Uncle Silas "peeled off one of his brilliant old-time blessings with as many layers as an onion ... whilst the angels hauled in the slack of it." No criminal stole prayer. Prayer died from exposure. Too many "Holy Joes" prostituted prayer in public. No sinner did it. It was self-appointed saints like Uncle Silas who kept dragging prayer out in front of everybody for a contest. Prayer died on pursed lips.

No wonder Christ condemned the social disease that "prayer bees" came to be, and commanded His disciples to pray privately. In a strangely powerful parable Jesus ridiculed the loud prayer of a prominent religious front-runner and praised the secret words of a spiritual nobody: "O Lord, have mercy on me a sinner" (*see* Luke 18:13).

However, people have prayer mixed up with Uncle Silas, so our time has put prayer to bed with a book. We pay professionals to nurse it, but they don't have to do it around the

15

clock. We have bent prayer for our football teams to use against each other. Prayer is what you do when there is no hope. It is an old hand-me-down that we've turned into "kid stuff" so they can show off just before dinner in front of company: "Jamie, will you say grace?" Is that why teenagers won't touch it? Is that why prayer has become a football for phonies and fanatics?

Is the world dying because prayer is a dying art? Are we at each other's throats because we can't hear God? Without God our accelerated program of education simply accelerates our descent into hell. Now we've jumped over the moon and can't find our way down to earth or up to heaven.

Prayer is life's largest order. No flip "Now I lay me down to sleep" can pull it off. Christ prayed all night, night after night, flat on His face in a garden, till great drops of blood appeared on His head. He prayed with His life close behind His prayer.

Prayer is an imperious art. Sometimes the door opens only to one who keeps on knocking. Prayer is a mystery. Prayer is a paradox. The One who hears our prayers before we ask Him did not heal the centurion's servant until he was at the door of death. Praying for someone may mean more than words and tears. Prayer may mean fasting; it may even mean dying.

A true pilgrim might approach prayer fearfully: "Talk me out of it!" And at the same time, eagerly: "Where do I start?" Dare listening. That's how Elijah heard the still small voice. Risk stargazing. That's how the wise men saw the star that lighted them to the dawn. Prayers are only pouts to Santa Claus or empty echoes in the air if you are afraid to look up high, or too proud to look down low enough to find a manger. Prayer may take a sacrifice of more than lamb. You must look out the window before you'll ever find much in the mirror. Friendships begin with introductions. God's first.

IF I COULD PRAY AGAIN

If I could pray
Again,
I think I would begin
The way my mother
Taught me—
Beside my bed.
But when I lay me
Down,
I find I can't go back:
The bridge is burned.
I can't go on like this;
The road ahead dead-ends.
My only hope is height.
And yet
I know of nothing new
For that, my Father,
Except to try once more—
Just as I used to do—
Asking inspiration
In this more pressing
Situation;
Remembering You promised
The Kingdom
To those becoming
Like little children once again.
And so I pray You, Lord,
Once more;
Teach me this time
My soul to keep
For others' sake,

As well as Christ's.
O let me sleep
And wake tonight
On that,
'Til prayer comes back
To me.

Before You Call I Will Answer

1

Before They Call I Will Answer

God is a bigger subject than prayer. God does better than go by the Book of Prayer. He created the world long before anyone thought to ask Him. He re-creates persons right and left around us now who have never even learned His name, and He often denies His truest saints pledged to ceaseless intercession.

The idea that the church has a monopoly on prayer is a grave mistake. Oftentimes those of us who have gotten into the habit of prayer oppose its power. Sometimes I think that the only pretext for our believing the Lord prefers the church is the Scripture that says, "The dead shall be raised first."

A friend of mine in her forties longed to be a nurse, but a medical checkup confirmed once again an unacceptable heart condition along with a long-standing heart murmur. Not long after this evaluation she attended an outdoor church service with her twenty-two-year-old daughter at a place in the Midwest called Quaker Valley. During the service someone sang, "He Touched Me." Suddenly she had a sensation of warmth in her chest and goose bumps all over her. It occurred to her that she was being healed. She nudged her daughter and whispered, "I think I'm being healed." Her daughter glared at her for disrupting the quiet and hissed, "Shush, you're in church."

As soon as she returned home, she eagerly reported her news to her husband. He responded, "I knew you were too tired for church tonight."

The next week she returned to the doctor who had formerly examined her. He examined her again. "Come back next week," he told her, "so that I may examine you once more." She did. After that examination the doctor declared, "I have not found any evidence of your heart condition or murmur in either of these last two examinations. It is my belief that God has healed you and that you ought to tell others."

Think of those who have prayed for someone else and the Lord has answered them instead. That nurse, for instance, had been praying for years, in vain, for her husband, who suffered from epilepsy. And I think of Mattie, who sat to my left one summer in a circle at Laity Lodge, the conference grounds of the Howard Butt Foundation near Kerrville, Texas. We were taking turns responding to the question "Do you care to share a time when you ran into God?" When Mattie's turn came, she related an incident that had happened a few years before.

Everyone in her family, she said, had suffered a hearing loss in mid-life. Several of her brothers had gone deaf and she had grown hard of hearing. She attended a healing service led by Kathryn Kuhlman that was held in a city within driving distance of her home. She remembered consciously praying for several noticeably wretched children near where she was seated.

Then she saw Miss Kuhlman pointing toward the section of the auditorium where Mattie sat. Over the loudspeaker Mattie faintly made out the words, "Someone over there is being healed in their hearing." "Almost immediately," said Mattie, "it seemed as though someone turned up the volume very loud. I have heard well ever since."

Anyone undertaking a study of prayer is soon faced with a God "whose rain falls on the just and the unjust," which means He cares for us whether or not we care for Him, or as it says in the Scripture that entitles this chapter, "And it shall come to pass, that before they call, I will answer..." (Isaiah 65:24).

God took on Joyce long before she took Him on. She is an attractive woman now who says her prayers, but she looks back to the time when she was ten when the Lord looked out for her without her prompting. Her father left. Her mother remarried, then died when Joyce was thirteen. Not long after the funeral her stepfather announced, "Joyce, I have seven kids to take care of on top of you. You will have to go." Little Joyce packed one battered bag.

That day she ran into an older teenage girl who let Joyce room with her. Joyce worked her way through high school, signing her father's name to her grade cards, living in mortal fear of being found out and forced into an orphanage. A teacher finally did discover her secret but promised not to tell; and when Joyce couldn't come up with the money to rent her cap and gown for graduation, that teacher came to her rescue.

A verse from the Psalms always comes to my mind when I think of Joyce. "When my father and my mother forsake me, then the Lord will take me up" (Psalms 27:10). You may have to write a letter to get Santa's attention. "Let me know if you ever need anything," says a friend. God is more sensitive. Often you don't have to apply.

Back when Joyce was ten, after her father had gone, but before her mother remarried, Joyce was little "Miss Fix-it" around the house. One morning when the coffee percolator was overheating, her little sister solicited Joyce's help. As Joyce leaned over the boiling pot, it blew up in her face. She was rushed to the hospital. The physicians treated her for severe third-degree burns on her face and neck.

As the emergency crew worked over the stricken child, they were awestruck by an inexplicable phenomenon. Around her eyes, which should have taken the full force of the explosion, was an unburned area that took the shape of an adult hand. Yet Joyce insisted that no adult was near her. Even her little sister had no warning to lift a tiny hand to protect her. How often God helps those who never had a chance, prayer or no prayer.

And so many examples come to my mind of God helping people who were trying to hurt Him. It is one thing for God to pick up an innocent child such as Joyce, but the annals of ministry tell of God coming to the defense of the guilty. This is not unscriptural. Did not the father of the prodigal son (*see* Luke 15) act before the boy could find the right words? And when the words came to that black sheep, did not the father interrupt his prayers to bestow upon him far more superior benefits than he had requested, to say nothing of deserved.

Just as I came in the door from work one day while this manuscript was underway, the phone rang:

> "Mr. Redding, you don't know me, but I am calling to thank you for your book *Jesus Makes Me Laugh,* which I have just finished hearing on a Library of Congress talking book. My name is Vernon Coldiron and I am calling from Chillicothe, Missouri. Do you have a minute?"

Mark Twain has written of how far an author would go for anyone who dares to pay such tribute. So, after such a comment my patience was certainly not at an end; but I was totally unprepared and am not yet recovered from the brief traumatic message that followed. The voice was serene, that of a young man, perhaps thirty, who had once been on active duty with the Green Berets.

> "Five years ago I worked for General Motors in Kansas City. I had an ulcer—caused or at least made worse by personal problems. I did not know God. My life was going from bad to worse. My doctor had prescribed two 10-mg Valium tablets a day. One day I felt terrible so I called in sick at work. I took four or five Valium, and according to my buddies, drank a lot of beer. It was open house at the plant and I easily walked in.

I went to my normal work station and into the foreman's office. The next thing my fellow workers saw was my foreman coming out of his office with his hands on his head—with me behind him with a gun in his back.

"I marched him upstairs and held him hostage for several hours. They cleared that section of the plant of all personnel and called in the Kansas City Police Support (SWAT) Team. I kept shouting out contradictory answers to their offers to negotiate. One time I indicated I would surrender my hostage in return for amnesty. Ten minutes later I asked for tobacco. Finally the police were ordered to shoot to kill. A bullet from one of those M 16's entered one-half inch below my right eye and came out my left temple.

"The paramedics worked over me in the ambulance but could get no pulse. Officially, I was 'dead on arrival' at the hospital. While the attendants were waiting for someone to come from the morgue, some ten to twenty minutes later, they heard screaming and found that I had returned to consciousness and had broken four restraining bands. The next day I went into a coma.

"When I came out of that coma over two months later, everything was dark. The voices over the loudspeaker finally made me realize that I was in a hospital and that the door to my room must be open. The lights in the hallway would not be out though. I was blind.

"Mr. Redding, you don't have to believe this, but the very next thing I realized was that I had been dead and had come back to life. I asked myself why I who had turned my back on the Lord wasn't dead and lost forever. And then I heard a voice—not my own, and there was no one else in the room—a warm and loving voice that told me that the Lord Jesus Christ, who had given himself that I might be saved, wanted to give me one more chance to be saved. That's all I needed to know and right then I accepted Jesus into my life. Now I'm living alone, yet I'm not alone, in my own apartment and calling you."

God helps people who not only do not help themselves but who hurt Him and themselves. Just as the church has no monopoly on God, neither does prayer. I believe in answered prayer, but because of such experiences as Vernon Coldiron's, I'm discovering so many answers that preceded prayer. God often jumps the gun and not only blesses the bread before grace is said, but also where no grace was intended, but evil instead.

Prayer is as often the result as it is the means of our blessings. Instead of praying our way into miracles, we often discover ourselves praying our way out of miracles.

And prayer works not only before we pray it, but also long after we thought God forgot; even after we forgot we ever prayed. He cares for us after we don't care anymore. God hears before we have grace enough to pray, and remembers to answer long after we have given up our final benediction.

Sons who have gone to hell come back. There is no hell beyond the reach of prayer. The One who "descended into hell" said, "With God nothing is impossible." Let's not get pathological with prayer; but even a graveyard reminds me that someone rose from the dead.

A son in our family got into trouble. He might well have concluded that he had been written off as noncollege material, when actually he was too far ahead of his class.

He was determined to take the fast lane, entering adolescence at age three or four, if the following episode is relevant. His mother was in the process of tugging him to a public rest room when he dug in his heels outside the door, and pointing to the words above the door asked, "What does that say?" She replied, "Women." He said, "I'm not supposed to go in there."

His mother turned him over to me and as we neared our door, he pointed above it and questioned, "What does that say?" I replied, "Men." He let go my hand and marched inside ahead of me. Surveying the row of his new colleagues lined up against the wall in front of him, he announced himself in a loud voice, "Hi, men."

He was a loveable and laughable comedian. But the elementary school felt he was squandering his great ability.

I suspected his junior-high-school truancy from his glowing tan, which I didn't think he acquired in class but likely resulted from his surfing, as we lived along the ocean. He and a friend also took over Disney World, which unfortunately was only an hour away, became skilled in cutting those tiny speedboats so as to douse onlookers with a sheet of water, and once repeatedly baptized two exasperated men dressed in tempting business suits who were attempting pursuit in a helpless sailboat.

As comical as his boyish pranks were, we decided it might be wise to scoop up our beachcomber and move to the country— though I realized later that surfing had developed a powerful swimmer; and those lonely vigils offshore gave him prime time to dream, and to gather the determination to do something with his life.

We moved to the country for a change. We had avoided motorcycles with the other boys, but "little irrepressible," who by now had become "big irreversible," managed to acquire the largest "trail bike" I ever saw. He and I promised his mother it would only be ridden on our farm.

He kept that promise. I did not. The day we moved up the hill to the new stone house I asked him if he would run an errand on his bike next door. It meant his going out on the state road. He had no license. He was only fifteen. He no sooner made the turn out of the lane and gunned it onto the highway than I heard the screech of tires and a collision. Along with the

collision I heard a noise like the cracking of a sapling. I raced
to him. He was lying beside the road, still astride the motorcycle; his leg, which I had heard break, almost torn off.

We were told later that the physicians were for amputation,
except for Dr. Kubiac, who reported to us late that night that
he had pieced it together the best he could. Now we would see.

He was in terrible pain, partly from fever due to an infection
that developed. He was allergic to penicillin and related drugs,
and there was a hole in his calf into which one could put an
egg. It would not heal.

Worst of all, whatever his faults, he had always been the one
to cheer the rest of us when we were down, with the smile that
wouldn't quit. That smile quit in the hospital. He turned his
face to the wall. We feared for his leg, finally for his life; but
nothing was as hard for me to take as having to face him without his smiling anymore.

One weekend found us in "the pits." I had to drive an hour
or so up the road from the hospital to preach a sermon as a
guest. You don't need medical bulletins to know when things
are bad for someone you love. I couldn't breathe. It was as
though I had a stone resting on my chest. Suddenly up in the
chancel, in front of everyone, I found myself weeping, and
wondering how I could ever preach; but I had to excuse the
spectacle I was making of myself, and finally got through the
service.

Afterward everyone went out of his way to reassure me of
his prayers; however, none of those well-wishers budged the
stone on my chest.

The last one in the reception line that day was a little retired
schoolteacher who took my hands in both of hers and said,
"Don't you worry. Your son will be all right." Immediately, in
a way I'll never understand, my stone was rolled away.

That night when I entered my son's hospital room, the floor
was covered and the air was filled with flying paper airplanes.

Two years later he skied as well as ever. He sailed through high school in three years.

He enrolled in a very demanding academic program at a university. Dedicated as he became, academic gaps plaguing his past were not plugged overnight.

His staying in the elite program hung on one advanced chemistry final lab exam. He had to have an "A" in that exam and in that course. Because of an accident he had had in that laboratory, his score in laboratory technique was in jeopardy. My son set up the complicated network of tubes and glassware for which the crucial experiment called. Then his arm inadvertently struck his setup and everything crashed to the floor.

Now in desperation, he ransacked the storeroom and came up with sufficient equipment, though it had not been cleaned and dehumidified, to assemble a second attempt. Just then the teaching assistant came by and announced, "You are too late getting started. Tear it down." "Yes, sir." Sometimes you have to give up, but as he started to dismantle his equipment he stopped and said to himself, "When have I ever gotten anywhere thinking like that." He realized that he was going against the T.A.'s orders, with only a slim chance of success since no one else's experiment was working either, but he leaned by his desk and prayed. "O God, if you would ever like to give me a hand, now would be a good time."

The laboratory T.A. had been working with a student directly behind Mark, hoping to have at least one successful experiment, then turned around to find that Mark's was doing beautifully. He was elated because no other experiments in the other sections under the other T.A.s were working either: "Mark, I'll stay with you through the dinner hour to finish it."

Later a girl's unit nearby went up in flames threatening the entire classroom. While everyone stood by paralyzed, my son swiftly smothered it with the only available fire extinguisher.

But as his demon might have it, the T.A. was temporarily out of the room and had to miss this timely heroism.

Mark not only received an "A" for the course, he was awarded (the T.A. somehow found out about the fire) the highest grade in the class for technique.

After an outstanding performance on the examinations required for admission, he was accepted in the school of medicine at a distinguished university. The other day he said something I still can't quite bring myself to say: "Dad, I thank God for that motorcycle accident."

Not only is it never too soon for God, let me encourage any reader who has a son or daughter, or a thief on a cross nearby, that it is never too late for God.

Prayer may fare best of all when it is forbidden. God not only gets to us before we pray and long after we've stopped, God is good at getting through when He's excluded.

How often we hear someone's excuse for not going to church, "I had too much Sunday school as a kid." Prayer dies when it is forced. Americans who never said a prayer in their lives began upon hearing it declared illegal in school by the Supreme Court.

Prayer thrives now behind the Iron Curtain in a way it does not in the free world. It is as though true prayer requires opposition. Put prayer in a popular easy chair and you'll pervert it. Prayer can survive only on some hard kneeling bench. And so Christ concludes His Beatitudes: "Blessed are those who are persecuted for righteousness' sake, for theirs is the kingdom . . ." (Matthew 5:10 RSV).

God hears best those who are not allowed to pray, those who refuse to pray, who don't deserve to pray, who forget to pray, or who pray after it's too late. This book is for people like that, for people like me who pray and who don't pray.

Before God ever created earth, and risked the cry that came from there, He had already determined that He could handle it. That cross would not be too big for Him to carry, nor the stone too large to roll away. He knew all along, as Christ sweat through Gethsemane and struggled up that last hill, that He would surely rise again; and when He repeated, "Let there be light," this time there would be light the darkness could not overcome. God had the answer long before Adam and Eve bothered about the apple.

LEND A HAND

O Lord, it is so hard
for those who cried all night
to bear our laughter.
How many have to suffer
through our smiles
for someone else,
when they've been out
of smiles so long
it isn't fair.
What's a hand to do
that's been dropped
and left hanging
all alone.
Shaking hands
is no solution.
Every hand needs a
hand to hold it.
Aren't there enough hands
to go around
until we circle at last
this lonely earth
and no one will be able
to make a fist anymore?

2

The Forge and the Anvil

Are you old enough to remember a smithy, the shop of a blacksmith? I can remember spending many hours as a boy in that enchanting place. In those days the smith not only shod horses, he fashioned whatever ironwork the farmer wanted. One French ironmonger told me that for admission to his craft he had to make a rose out of one piece of metal. He proudly showed it to me.

Our blacksmith was not only the strongest man in town, he was the most ingenious. He worked magic with metal. It seemed to me, as I watched that bearded giant hammer out chains and hinges from scraps of blazing iron, with the smoke hanging from the ceiling and sparks like falling stars flying from his blows, that I was watching God work miracles. I still think so.

There were two major components to qualify a shop as a smithy: an anvil and a forge. A blacksmith would never think of trying to shape cold iron on the anvil before he had heated it white-hot in the forge. By pumping the bellows he could make his forge far hotter than any stove. And fresh from the forge the orange iron was almost as malleable as clay.

Ever try to bend cold iron by hammering it on the anvil? Any blacksmith would tell you that hell is filled with people trying to do that. You'll lose your religion trying to bend cold iron.

35

That is what has happened to us. Life is like a great black-smith shop with an overworked anvil and an overlooked forge. We feature the arm and hammer and have forgotten fire.

I see the anvil as the symbol of work and the forge as the symbol of prayer. And we respect hard work and suspect soft prayer. We like to solve problems by working on them rather than by being worked on. We wear our pants out in the seat, not in the knees. We're not busy putting legs on prayers, just putting legs on more legs. We don't have too many irons on the fire, we have too many irons on the anvil.

There is a winsome painting still hanging in many homes of a farmer and his wife in the old country standing in a potato field with folded hands and bowed heads. The spade and wheelbarrow are put aside while the couple pauses in response to the peal of the Angelus that has rung from a church spire visible in the distance.

Such a sight at the roadside now would stop cars. No couple could pray outdoors now for the flashbulbs of photographers frantic to capture such a quaint oddity on film.

The church herself has antiquated the forge and honored the anvil. The minister is fortunate to finish his dessert let alone wait upon the Lord. Churches covet a preacher who is a go-getter rather than a man of God. If some minister claimed to spend much time in prayer, it would arouse the suspicions of a pulpit search committee.

We still vaguely refer to the church as the house of prayer, but when someone calls upon us for the church we know what is wanted—money. Even if the caller or the TV program is clever enough to postpone mentioning it, no one is out simply soliciting and dispensing prayers. When the church meets it means business. We are oriented to consider what we can do for the church, not what the church can do for us.

Did the fire go out in the forge? Are prayers forced now from cold ashes? We've been going to the anvil lukewarm and unbending. Our attempts at conversion have been descending into strong-arming. Are we trying to rush it—too immature to wait in the forge for that mighty wind we cannot manufacture?

Surely we won't give up the forge just because we've lost its art. That would be far more foolish than to surrender electricity because we short-circuited its power.

Martin Luther said he prayed twice as long when he had twice as much to do. Dead tired after a long day of Parliament Prime Minister William Gladstone was said to sigh, "I'm so exhausted I'm going straight to church."

We speak of getting psyched for a test. Can we comprehend the astonishing action of the forge in this light?

Queen Esther was a Jewish wife of King Ahasuerus of Persia. His trusted friend, Mordecai, was also a Jew; but a calculating villain named Haman, to strengthen his position with the king and weaken Mordecai's, persuaded the king unwittingly to approve an edict that would cause the massacre of all the Jews in the land.

Mordecai told Esther that she was the only one who could save them. She must go to the king and intercede for her people. Even then it would take a miracle, for the Persians prided themselves on "the king's word that cannot be broken."

However, in those times you did not just jump up and run to the king about something. If he had not requested your company, he could turn his golden scepter down upon your interruption, and that would be your last interruption. Besides, the king had a number of influential wives, and he had not sent for Esther for a long time.

So Esther was not anxious to beard the royal lion. However, Mordecai strengthened her resolve by suggesting that if the slaughter of the Jews succeeded, her current favor with the king would not be enough to save her. Then he added, ". . .who knoweth whether thou art come to the kingdom for such a time as this?" (Esther 4:14).

Esther gathered her courage and in one of the bravest deci-sions anyone ever made she agreed, saying ever so eloquently, ". . . if I perish, I perish" (Esther 4:16).

Before heading for her anvil to do what had to be done, she retired to the forge. She requested every Jew in Persia to fast for her for the three days before she went to the king. And by the time she made her request to the king, he was defenseless: "What wilt thou, queen Esther? . . . it shall be even given thee to the half of the kingdom" (Esther 5:3).

The forge does not stand for spoken prayers necessarily; it signifies waiting in God's presence, soaking up His warmth. We do not affect the forge so much as it affects us. It signifies being affected by an unbelievably hygienic and nourishing atmo-sphere, such as happens with plants sunning themselves.

In prayer a light "brighter than the sun" comes on, as Saint Paul said happened to him en route to Damascus. Perhaps its effect is something like the effect our favorite song or poem has upon us; or what it means to be sitting beside our favorite friend; what it does to a baby to bask in his mother's arms.

What happens to a person when he falls in love? No one knows the extent of the curative powers, the dynamic effect on the will to live in such an experience. Consider the effect of falling in love with God. What does it do to have someone so creative, so life-giving, take your breath away? Such an inti-macy with God rests and tunes the heart. There is a bath we call a baptism. There is a breath so strong, Scripture refers to it as "a mighty wind," where "tongues of fire" have been known to fall on everyone present in prayer.

Christ did not leap into His ministry and begin pounding on pulpits and banging heads together. As soon as He was bap-tized He retreated into the wilderness for forty days and forty nights. What a switch that was! What a forge!

After that experience, not before, He had power to bend ears back into shape. Then miracles flew from His fingers and fell from His clothes. Tongues were untied at a glance, backs straightened with a whisper. Jesus didn't have to beat on people. They were putty in His hands. His touch was light, but worked like lightning. It was all because He had bathed in the furnaces of God.

Christ's ministry began and ended in prayer. He got something from prayer we have missed. As much as Christ accomplished, we never think of Him as a hard worker or a busy man. He made it look so easy and as though He had all the time in the world, all because of this secret forge.

The transfiguration of our world, and our lives, will not come by threats of another flood, nor advice, nor by force. We will never get to where we need to be simply by working on each other. We need to be welded and that will take fire.

BEFORE I CALLED

Your sunlight is something else
since we've been under a cloud so long.
Perhaps it takes a prisoner
to appreciate freedom,
a loser to love victory,
and people who have been astray
to be eager to find the Way,
the Truth, and the Life.

Fervently do we pray,
that it won't be necessary
for us to have to get hurt
to enjoy health, or to
lose an eye to be glad
for the other one.
Forbid that our loved ones
will have to be taken away from us
before we find how dear they are.

Keep us from taking anything
for granted,
from depreciating what we have
by always wanting more.
Teach us how to take everything
with love
so we can give something
with power
as He did with glory.

3

Your Prayer Is What You Really Want

Augustine's prayer, "O God, make me good, but not just now," may be wrong, but it's true. Preachers pray so politely, it's seldom honestly. We tell God what we think He wants to hear, not what we really want to say. So prayer dies from telling those little white lies with such careful thees and thous.

We approach Christ as though we were having our picture taken—not for the X ray that it is. So our grace before dinner no more sets forth our true feelings about the burned potatoes and our churning intestines than the ancient creed of the Ukranian Orthodox Snow Festival. Here we are, in agony, and we think we're supposed to say something nice, as though prayer were an unrelated exercise in ecclesiastical etiquette. One can take God's name in vain in prayers.

We race through the Lord's Prayer as though saying, "Pass the butter," to the moon. We say, "Thy kingdom come on earth as it is in heaven," but we've been more excited by a day off. We take prayer so lightly we cannot remember what we prayed for last Sunday.

Bad words are better than phony words. Telling God off would be better than kidding Him. Read the Psalms. Some of them address God almost savagely, but they are real. The psalmist takes prayer to be a time when he can let down his hair—let the cat out of the bag. Only then can he manage an honest "hallelujah."

On the cross Christ Himself quoted from the Twenty-second Psalm, which begins with the shocking question Christ used: "My God, my god, why hast thou forsaken me?" That psalm is crammed with the most uncomplimentary remarks about this life. It is not only a moan from the pits, it registers a strong objection to the universe: "Our fathers trusted in thee ... and thou didst deliver them. . . . but I am a worm, and no man . . . . all they that see me laugh . . ." (Psalms 22:4–7).

The psalm ends on a more positive note, but its brutal frankness reflects the reckless daring of biblical devotion. Good men confess the murder in their hearts, the black thoughts that bury them, and they fling them in God's face. There is no fooling in the great prayers of the Bible.

Your prayers are not always what you say they are, but rather what you are yearning for. Your true prayer is revealed by the direction you are leaning. God does not read lips, so we must stop "fooling ourselves with trivial devotions" as Brother Lawrence damned it. The Lord is not into cosmetics; He is something like a cardiologist. He notices what races our pulse, what raises our blood pressure.

James Montgomery wrote:

> Prayer is the soul's sincere desire
> Unuttered or expressed;
> The motion of a hidden fire
> That trembles in the breast.

And since prayer is our longing, everybody prays. We may not pray the right way to the right God, but so long as someone is looking for something, or counting on something, that is praying. One need not kneel or count beads on a rosary, or say a word, to be praying.

Edison's obsession to find a filament for his light bulb, Macbeth's ambition to be king, Schweitzer's zeal to heal Africa were prayers. You might say that praying doesn't even require belief in God. So long as one is after something, such as breath, then in the very deepest sense one is praying.

In this fundamental sense one can pray to the devil. The Pharisee prayed to himself according to Jesus' parable. People pray in their worst hours as well as their noblest.

Harry Emerson Fosdick, in his classic, *The Meaning of Prayer,* saw that life's disasters are not due to unanswered prayers. Trouble so often comes because we are asking for it— we were driving too fast, or on the wrong side of the road, on a curve, on ice.

In Psalm One Hundred and Six we read, "He gave them their request; but sent leanness into their soul." David Head took that for the title of his refreshing book on prayer. The tragedy as well as the comedy in this life has to do with people getting exactly what they prayed for.

The Duke of Orange told his sons as they sailed toward Northern Ireland that the portion of land that included the beautiful harbor would belong to the son who touched it first. One son cut his hand off and threw it ashore. He got the harbor, and it maimed him. Faust's dreams came true in return for his soul's damnation. The throne that Macbeth craved fell on him. The prodigal son got his faraway country, and King Ahab got his bloody vineyard. Even Judas Iscariot was paid in full, thirty pieces of silver.

Your dreams will come true. We are all self-fulfilling prophesies. The fellow who is after social approval will get it, perhaps in the face, and at the expense of some other things. We so often make the grade we have set for ourselves; which, of course, requires our nailing other things to a cross. Jesus wrote the epitaph of such lives when He sighed, "I tell you they have their reward." Prayer is dangerous and easily perverted.

What consumes our attention finally gets us. What gets our attention? Moses watched a bush burn. He got so absorbed he began burning too, till men could not bear to stare him in the face (*see* Exodus 34:29, 30). God caught Moses' attention. And Moses got carried away—to God.

We learn to want God's will by keeping our eyes on Him. Tennyson tells of Arthur knighting his men. Every eye is on Arthur. They are pale, shaken, as though they have seen a ghost: "Suddenly through all their order flashed a momentary likeness of their king."

The hymn "Jesus Keep Me Near the Cross" says it for us: "Bring its scenes before me." That does it. No wonder the centurion was awestruck on Calvary. He stayed too long by that cross to stay the way he was. The mob stampeded from that hill. Everyone had to leave—or give up to Him. You can only bear to look at Christ for so long in derision, particularly near the Cross.

TO A QUICK CHANGE ARTIST

O Lord Jesus Christ
Deliver me from my schemes
To outwit what you want.
Forbid my life should go by and all I ever did
Was try to get the biggest piece of cake.
Teach me quickly how, "He who will save his life
Will lose it:"
Lest I be embarrassed in that final hour.
Give me something better to do,
Something that is more fun and more important,
Than self-service.
Help me to see the folly of my
Racing up the ladder faster than the other fellow
By remembering the One who took up His Cross
and went straight to the foot.
O God, this trying forever to get something
Is what gets me;
He gave Himself away.
That gets me right where He wants me.

Keep me Father from twisting your church
to my own advantage.
I arrange the hour to suit myself;
I make my gifts tax deductible.
Before you know it I'll have Christianity rigged
Until I have everything to gain
When You had everything to lose.
Take my hands out of my pockets
Until I can stretch them out before me
To heal and bless all I meet.

My time is running out
I need a quick change artist.
If I were the wind, I would obey You instantly.
Why not just as I am.

4

Prayer Is Play

Have you ever seen a baby trying to catch sunbeams? Perhaps you don't remember back that far, but playing was probably the first thing you ever did. You took a stick and it turned into a wand, or a gun, or a snake. Outside there was plenty of mud for pies, and inside there was enough paper to scissor for a month. You could build a city with a few blocks or drill an army with the fuzzies under the bed. Even little Bill Cosby, living in the inner-city projects, submerged himself in the water tank above the commode and played submarine. He would flush it and cry, "Let her rise! Let her rise!" The bathroom was his sandbox, and he mastered it, finally flushing down his father's overcoat successfully.

Play is what you cannot wait to do as soon as you get home from school or work. It is fooling around for the fun of it. A professional is one who does something because he is paid. Amateur refers to one who does something because he loves to. Play means joining the festivities until you enjoy *re*-creation. Play is the context of laughter and of prayer.

You are never too old to play. I don't mean a hobby you take up with some ulterior motive such as health. Play is what you delight in doing for its own sake. Dancing? Shopping? Doodling? Surfing? Hot-rodding? What have *you* done since hopscotch? Colonel Sanders was said to enjoy following famous people around.

Work can become play. One man said about his business,

"I'm like a dolphin in the ocean. I love it." My father accomplished this magic for me. He never forced me to work on the farm that we moved to in my teens. His affection for farming was so contagious it became my sandbox.

My father had Tom Sawyer's knack for enticing you into whitewashing the fence. Remember how Aunt Polly plagued Tom to death about painting that fence? Finally Tom devised a plan. When the carefree gang came by to torment poor Tom for being stuck in hard labor all day Saturday, they were shocked to see Tom savoring each stroke, so carried away by the ecstasy of whitewashing that he acted as though he didn't even know they were there. Before long everybody was begging to help. Reluctantly, Tom yielded before the pressure of high-priced keepsakes. Tom was paid aggies, toads, and fishhooks for the privilege of painting Aunt Polly's fence. Tom psyched everybody into thinking it was play.

Play can be perverted, as it was when Roman soldiers gambled beneath the cross for Christ's clothes. Playing jokes on someone at his expense is what it means to be a bad sport. Games can become gods that sap life. Play is more than playing poker, or taking a trip, or hallucinating.

Competition can overpower play. Tennis can turn into torment if you never win. All losers become poor losers after a while, and victory is not always so sweet for the ego. Play degenerates if it becomes exclusively a matter of someone beating someone else.

Spectator sports leave something to be desired. Our professional pastimes are a beautiful part of our way of life; the tragedy comes when spectatoritis absorbs creative play. Rome fell while the sports fans were sitting there in the Coliseum drooling over spectacles. They called those shows live, but they helped kill the people. There are good books, but one can become a bookworm. There are good television shows, but one can become a tube boob.

A *Time* magazine (January 12, 1976) article on television soap operas reported: "A few years ago CBS was obliged to eliminate soap opera characters who were poor because the network was receiving piles of care packages, and the endlessly frustrated romance of Alice Matthews and Steve Fram drove fans of 'Another World' crazy. 'Why don't you let them get married?' wailed one viewer. 'Four times I've bought a wedding dress for the wedding—four times I've bought champagne.' At Princeton something like a quarter of the student body dropped everything to watch 'The Young and the Restless' each afternoon."

Television in moderation can be relaxing and entertaining. But there comes a time when we are no longer playing TV; it is playing us. How many times have I felt too rotten about the outcome of a game a thousand miles away to have time to care for someone nearby?

Nothing must rob us of real play, for all work and all artificial play not only make Jack a dull boy, but make him deadly serious. We cannot afford to lose the capacity to entertain ourselves unassisted. Paul Tournier claims you can predict a child's later adult happiness and success by whether he is able to entertain himself alone.

Father Christopher Mooney claims that "Man only plays when he is human, and is only human when he plays. . . . Civilization arises and unfolds only as play in its interpretation and proceeds to mold and shape man before it is defined as a form of cultural order. . . . Play gets rid of fixations, moralisms, self-righteousness. . . . Ritual festivity is man's highest moment. . . . Play offers freedom from pressure—freedom from everyday living. Play is living on the frontier of your imagination."[1]

Christianity likes to play. As we shall see in the next chapter, "Anyone who will not receive the kingdom of God like a little child will never enter it" (Mark 10:15 NIV). Christ could have

[1] Notes from an address delivered in Kansas City, May, 1975.

condemned us to hard labor; but instead it's like going fishing. "Come, follow me, and I will make you fishers of men." Some religions required days walking on coals of fire and nights lying on beds of spikes, but "My yoke is easy, My burden is light." Jesus said, "We piped for you, and you would not dance." Jesus was accused of being a glutton and a winebibber. They assaulted Him: "Why don't your men fast?" He replied, "How can they fast when the Bridegroom is still with them?" He identified himself as a bridegroom. His parables were filled with feasts and comedy. The return of the prodigal still shocks the world. There was no punishment; "There was the sound of music and dancing." A bad boy came back, and it set the house afire with festivity. Pharisees solemnly levied the complicated commandments necessary; it was a lot of work. Jesus had men laying down their lives eagerly to please Him.

We have long been accustomed to thinking of church as a requirement instead of a reward. We urge each other to pray and read our Bibles until, before we know it, we have twisted the blessing into a burden. It is no longer "Good News"; it has become more chores to do in an already overworked life. Instead of the relief Christ promised, church becomes our responsibility. Instead of the rock holding us up, we are holding up the rock.

Has prayer become one of your good works? Do you pray because you ought to—or because you have more fun with God than with anyone else?

Obviously prayer can be hard. Prayer can be Gethsemane. But think about prayer from God's point of view. He's your Father. You're His child. Would you like your child to come to you only because he knows he ought to? Would you appreciate your child writing you letters and visiting you because he disciplined himself to do it?

When the prodigal came home, the father didn't send him back to school. He didn't put him to work or punish him. He celebrated! Having his son back was like having a party. What would please the heavenly Father more than to have you feel that festive about going out with Him? The Westminster Catechism says, "The chief end of man is to glorify God and enjoy Him forever." When do we start?

Creation was not hard work to God, nor was the re-creation at Pentecost. They said it was a breeze. There was no drudgery in the Garden. It was after Adam fell and was forced to leave Eden that women went into labor and men began to sweat. Christ's miracles were called works but they were not manufactured. They happened—like walking on water. You cannot classify your conversion as the culmination of your good deeds. It is by God's grace, "That no man may boast." "It is a gift."

Perhaps the Lord does us the way Charles Schulz does "Peanuts," or the way Michelangelo let *David* out of the stone. Re-creation is like creation. It is recreation. As Plato said, "Man is a plaything in the hands of God." He made us to begin with, as though from mud pies. Your re-creation today may seem at first like a sand castle in the air. "Now do me, God." "If You want to You could make me well." "Of course I want to. Be healed."

The playing is not finished when we come down to the door of death. One would think that if God did play with us as a cat plays with a mouse, death would be an end to it. But no magician can compare with the Master, particularly in the finishing touch of play with which He surprises us. The hand that is quicker than the eye brought the mutilated body of Christ back to more beautiful life. He does the last event in style. He beats every one of us at our own game. He makes it look so easy. I mean His loving us in the midst of the ugly way they worked Him over. He didn't complain about dying: "But like a lamb led before his shearers is dumb, so He opened not His mouth" (*see* Acts 8:32). It would seem He had a bitter end that He took hard, but we are also told that "It was for the joy that was set before Him that Christ endured the Cross" (*see* Hebrews 12:2). Dying over the heads of those gambling Roman soldiers was Someone who knew how to play the game.

This is not unrealistic. Orville Kelly was informed some years ago that he had terminal cancer. He and his wife went home to cry—to die. Should they keep it secret? They prayed. The answer was that they should play about it. So they decided to put on a big party. They invited all their friends. During the festivities, Orville held up his hand to make an announcement: "You may have wondered why I called you all together. This is a cancer party. I have been told I have terminal cancer. Then my wife and I realized we are all terminal. We decided to start a new organization. It is called M.T.C.—'Make Today Count.' You are all charter members."

Since that time the organization has spread across the country. Orville pointed out the way we Christians are to play into the jaws of death—singing, loving, not losing a minute from "the joy the world cannot give nor take away."

FORGIVE US FOR PRAYING

Forgive us our Father,
For the bad habit of praying
When it doesn't do any good,
Or make any difference to us.

How could we do this
To the fellowship of fire?
Joshua made the sun
Stand still.
Moses split the sea
In two.
One word from Christ and
The fever fled,
The storm died, and
Lazarus got out of his grave
Like getting out of bed.

Forgive us for the way
We bore people to death
Trifling with prayer.

5

Children Only

Prayer is not simply something mastered by the saints and the experts; it is a secret of childhood. One might assume that it would take a learned theologian, deep in some distinguished seminary, to tell us about so advanced a subject as talking to God. No. Better ask some child.

We still think children are supposed to go to school to learn from us old folks, but Jesus turned this around. He was not only not ashamed of His lack of formal education, He respected His juniors. What He was looking for was hidden in the hearts of bright-eyed little folk not yet adulterated.

It might be difficult for us to envision a department of religion chaired by a four-year-old, but this chapter is devoted to the neglected wisdom that comes "out of the mouths of babes and sucklings." George Bernard Shaw was calling for more modesty from adulthood when he said: "The only time my education was interrupted was when I was in school." This was something of the same attitude of the little six-year-old when her mother asked how it went on her first day at school: "Fine, except for some older lady who kept interrupting us."

Children are not only able to believe anything, they are able to love anyone. The longer we stay on earth, the further we get from the truth. Age saps our spiritual vitality. The facts we acquire seem to obscure the light of all our seeing. We become farsighted or nearsighted, so we need a child to take our hand.

A prominent educator said that if he enters a room full of

kindergartners and asks: "Children, do you love your teachers?" every single hand instantly goes up. But if he were to ask that question of the eleventh graders they would scorn: "Are you kidding, man." Something has been lost by then that we want back if we're ever to speak and listen to God.

Here I am writing a book on prayer that will be inexcusably deficient unless I can somehow sit at the feet of little children. And perhaps this will encourage them to be themselves and not to grow up too soon, not to play "grown-ups" too much, not to allow adults to organize all their games, or to kill their joy.

We're planning a children's sermon in our church where the children will preach to the preacher. My father confessed he was once stumped by the passage of Scripture where it speaks of Enoch being taken to heaven without having to die. And a little girl answered, "I know how it was. You said that Enoch walked with God every day. I think he walked a little farther each day until one day God said, 'Today, Enoch, you are closer to my home than we are to yours. Come on home with me.' "

While children must be taught to mind and to learn from us we must also mind them, so we turn to our little superiors for the finer points of prayer.

> Dear God,
> Please count me in.
> Your friend,
> Herbie

My young teenage friend Booger was already on old man in many ways, but his was a prayer of a child again. It came as a shock that day in church but left us with a blessing.

> O God, bless all the men here with long hair
> And all those with short hair,

> And all those with no hair, and help them to
> Love each other for Christ's sake.

Adults struggle laboriously up the ladder of prayer, like Jacob wrestling with the angel, but children fly to God. We see their wings in the giving as well as the taking aspect of prayer. Booger became a leader in the YMCA in St. Augustine where he used to break windows. He sponsored a basketball team of nine-year-olds that included a five-year-old boy who had no big toes, so couldn't pivot to play the game. His name was Herkimer Charles Bledsoe. He always wore the same shirt with the same big hole in the side, and he always carried his prize possession, a miniature tin replica of Artoo Detoo from *Star Wars.*

Someone stole their basketball, so Booger organized a can collection drive to make money to buy another. He stored the proceeds in an old sock. Herk, however, was too small to reach up into the Dempsey dumpster and look for cans. One day Booger poured out the contents of the sock to see if they had enough. Out came Artoo Detoo. And from that outpouring of a child's heart there poured out of the pockets of friends of mine at Liberty Church and Booger himself the money for the surgery that found Herk's toes waiting to emerge from his feet as good as new.

Children not only teach us how to pray, they come up with answers from God. Annie Pinney has permitted me to share the experience of her mother when she was a little girl. This heartwarming story not only illustrates how practical prayer is, it provides a parable. It is a child's demonstration of prayer lived out.

The heat was stifling inside the high stone walls of the courtyard. It was the summer of 1917 and war was raging all over France.

Suzanne sat on a wooden chair under the big acacia tree rocking her doll, her legs barely touching the ground. The letter had arrived from the front several days before, "Coming home at last, I love you all so much, Papa." Her mother had cried and Suzanne, not sure of what she should do in such circumstances, had cried along with her.

She did not like being six years old too much. Her brothers, ten and twelve, almost men now, went every day to work at the war plant with her mother. There was no one to keep her during the day and Mama cried sometimes when she left for work. But Suzanne could take care of herself; there were chores to do around the house and she was not allowed to go outside.

For the last seven days Suzanne had disobeyed Mama. She had waited for the big iron gate to close. Then she would run to the tall oak armoire, climb on a chair, and pull out her Sunday dress. The blue ribbon in her hair was Suzanne's prized possession. It was the same blue as Mary's dress in the big cathedral. Papa would have a princess to come home to. She knew exactly what she would do when he arrived; she had dreamed about it every day in the courtyard.

Suzanne had been very little when her father had left for the war, almost two years now, and she could not remember his face. But she looked at his picture every day. He was so magnificent in his cavalry uniform, holding his shining helmet with the long horsetail, a gleaming saber by his side; and she loved his mustache. He looked so strong, the way a papa should look. Every day she would polish the frame and reverently spit on the glass to make it shine. Then she would lay her favorite blue ribbon in front of it. It was her gift to him.

Suzanne shifted uncomfortably on her chair and pulled at her black cotton stockings; Mama insisted that respectable ladies always wore stockings. . . . She was hungry too, in fact she was always hungry. Sometimes they would have some bread and vegetables to eat, but more often they all went to bed hungry.

The heat made her tired, her eyelids were heavy; she yawned. The little doll fell in the dirt. She had not heard the gate open. The soldier was standing still, looking at her. His uniform was torn and covered with dust; she saw tears streaming down his bearded face. He was old. Fear suddenly made her stomach hurt the same way she felt when she heard the guns; she would hide under the bed then.

She was going to die, she probably would never see her family again, and Papa would not find her when he finally came home. She swallowed very hard and looked at the enemy, "Are you going to kill me?" she whispered.

The soldier had fallen on his knees in the dirt, his head down on his chest. A strange sound came from his throat. Suzanne did not know what to do. "You see," he said softly, "I am looking for a little girl just like you. I have not seen her in a very long time; I am her Papa."

That night they all clung to each other in Mama's big bed. Suzanne on one side, Mama on the other, and Papa in the middle, the boys at their feet. Suzanne had tied herself to her father's wrist with the blue ribbon. A father felt so good and warm. She was afraid to fall asleep; he might go away.

In the morning, Suzanne folded the blue ribbon carefully in a wooden cigar box and buried it deeply in the flower garden. As long as no one knew where it was, Papa would always stay with her. It was her secret forever. And she would never tell.

Second childhood is almost synonymous now with senility, but the Scripture insists that each grown-up's only hope is in somehow recovering that youthful longing to be bound by a blue ribbon to a Father. "Unless you become like a little child you cannot enter the kingdom."

What did Jesus mean? The idea mystifies us as it did Nicodemus: "Can a man return to his mother's womb for the second time?" (*see* John 3:4). But the childlikeness of a little Suzanne must be ours if we are ever to inherit this legacy of love. There is a God-shaped vacuum in the heart of each of us that takes our dressing up, our longing passionately, and our waiting forever in our own courtyard, no matter what—till He comes.

I swear it happened ever so clearly to my aged godmother. Aunt Alice was like my second mother and always beloved to me. However, those who knew her couldn't have missed her prejudices against strangers, foreigners, and anyone who deviated slightly from her politics. She never married, and this spirit of independence ruled out any need of a special handout from God, thank you. God was a formality to her. He was an austere ancestor to be respected, but not to be taken advantage of. Prayers were for putting legs on. She was a take-charge, no-nonsense nurse who had definitely grown up and out and away from any childlike faith.

However, when she finally consented to move next door to us, she fell and broke her good hip. She was eighty-four. The tower of strength who always nursed the rest of us needed nursing now. After a few days she wondered why she was not helped to her feet. Then we told her that that would require surgery on the other hip—at some risk. "Well," she said with the proud old spirit, "I can't stay like this. Go ahead." She made it safely through the operation but, as so often happens after surgery to older folks, she did not return mentally to her old self. Like almost all the rest of the older patients in the convalescent center, her mind drifted into that state that we refer to as second childhood. Aunt Alice as I knew her was no more.

I have noticed how often some people abandon their elders too quickly to this condition; just as others cling pathologically to unrealistic possibilities. What should I do? Days dragged by. I believe God suggested this to me. I could not be God. I could not even be very good, but I could at least listen to this suggestion: See her every single day if only for twenty minutes and repeat three things: "As soon as you can walk to the bathroom, we'll go home. I love you very much. See you tomorrow."

Before long she began singing this song and dance with me, finally smiling. It went on two months. One day she began reading the Psalms even before her mind came back. Then *Reader's Digest*—cover to cover. Soon she was her old self. No, she was not. Her independence had been broken. She was as clear as ever but clearly different. A spirit of thanksgiving and appreciation that she had not shown before overcame her. Some enemy of hers would have said she had been opinionated and prejudiced. But something happened to that crusty heart.

She still couldn't stand and walk. She was flunking therapy. Then another miracle. The therapist happened to be an angel who divined what Aunt Alice wanted. The reason she couldn't stand was that the chair arms were too high for her to get leverage. She was put in a higher chair with lower arms and stood almost immediately. Each day she showed off to me, strutting her first few steps, learning to walk all over again. A miracle she had taken for granted. Me too.

Some of us are glib with our faith. We talk a good faith. Not that old New York aunt of mine. One day she said a mouthful for her. She said something she had never in all her life said before. She said, looking up, words I never thought to hear from her, "I asked God to help me." She paused and wept, then added, "and He did." Her infirmity was the card God played to bring her to the manger. She fell toward heaven.

The woman who could never be helped was helped. She went back to her apartment, lived alone again as she wished, and worked every single day unpacking trunks and packages. One trunk she unpacked had been packed fifty years before. Day after day she worked putting her antique buttons on cards to get ready for the opening day of her long-planned shop. Her will was broken, not her spirit.

She couldn't bend down and pick up anything by hand, but she learned to use a grabber, a pole with pincers on the end. One day she spilled her pills and instead of waiting for me, she pinched up all fifty-six tiny heart pills by herself. She must have put in the afternoon doing it.

She didn't lose all her starch. One afternoon she anticipated a long talk, and I explained I had to run. She exploded, "Well, that's what you do best." But then she asked me to forgive her, something she could never do before. She lived till eighty-six for a reason.

One day when I came to see her she announced, "I want to tell you how your grandfather (her father) died." Immediately I sensed she was into sharing something she had never mentioned before. I could tell she was deeply moved. It was to be a blue-ribbon event.

"He was only forty-eight," she said, "but he had been dying from cancer all summer. He was lying in the front room with no complaints. He had been very brave. One day he called in the family and all the men from the fields. Even your great-grandfather came. Everyone stood hushed, in answer to his summons. Then very quickly in a strong voice he said, 'Come quickly, Lord Jesus,' and died."

Not long after, Aunt Alice died. Did not the Father waken her, too, sleeping there like a little child again in her best dress?

This can happen to you and me. Mother Teresa, in *Words to Love By* (Ave Maria Press, 1983), tells how this unbelievable change in attitude happens in the toughest experience. A hardened grown-up goes out and comes in all over again.

Once a lady came to me in great sorrow and told me that her daughter had lost her husband and a child. All the daughter's hatreds had turned on the mother. She wouldn't even see the mother. So I said, "Now you think a little bit about the things that your daughter liked when she was a child. Maybe flowers or a special food. Try to give her some of these things without looking for a return."

And she started doing some of these things, like putting the daughter's favorite flowers on the table, or leaving a beautiful piece of cloth for her.

Several days later the daughter said, "Mommy come. I love you. I want you."

It was very beautiful.

By being reminded of the joy of childhood, the daughter reconnected with her family life. She must have had a happy childhood to go back to the joy and happiness of her mother's love.

"Unless you become as a child you cannot enter the kingdom." When we do, our children will too.

A STOPPING PLACE

Father, I'm running as fast as I can,
But I'm falling farther behind.
I'll never catch up,
Unless You run to me.
That's why I'm waiting here at
This stopping place.
My days are gone before dawn,
The years fly by like dreams and
I'm scattered in the dust.
That's not so bad, for I'm done for
Running, without the advantage
Of Your hand—
Which I can never seem to find
In a hurry.
Since I'm a runner you'll have to show me
How to rest.
I suffer from drumming fingers
And tapping feet.
Teach me how to hold still
Like a baby being born,
So you can deliver me
Into a new world.
Then I'll know
Not that I'm so good, but
That You're God.

6

If It's No Fun, It's No Good

Pseudo-praising God can be pretty deadly. Many of the ways I've seen people do it—and been party to—make me sick. Surely God abhors the way the electric organ wails "Abide With Me" on the weary recording over the loudspeaker static at the funeral home. That's one awful way to say "thanks a lot" to God.

My Baptist preacher friend made everybody say "Amen" when he came to our church, as though that was it. My Aunt Glo was a member of a "Holiness" sect. To be saved only was elemental. She had been, as everyone in her church who was anyone had been, sanctified. And her presentation of her experience always upstaged all the rest. She dragged me with her, as a small boy, to her tent meetings.

One evening a man gave so eloquent a testimony about his deliverance from alcohol and his sanctification that I felt sure Aunt Glo had been silenced forever, but I underestimated the old superstar. She ascended a bench and announced, "I've not only been sanctified, I've been glorified," then whirled around and swooned headlong. That maintained her stratospheric position very adequately in my judgment. Although there was one small boy present that evening who had an even more ultimate experience. I was mortified.

As bizarre as Aunt Glo's performance was, she never bored me. While she may have usurped more than her share of the spotlight, at least she prayed creatively, which cannot always be said of Presbyterians who are often grimly determined to do whatever has to be done "decently and in order." Episcopalians, too, are not always electrifying, although it was one of their number who was persuaded God preferred them because the Scripture clearly states that "The dead shall be raised first."

Others insist that the way to praise God is to sprinkle your conversation frequently with the phrase "Praise the Lord." Some say you must do it kneeling, others that you have to raise your hands in the air.

My mother's people, in sharp contrast to my father's sister, my Aunt Glo, were Upstate New York United Presbyterians. According to them the only words God liked to hear were psalms, and they were to be sung without any instrumental accompaniment. The installation of the new pipe organ split the church. And the day the new minister insisted that a violinist take part, the song leader retaliated, "We will now fiddle and sing Psalm 119," which must have taken forty-five minutes, as that psalm has 176 verses.

The public praise of God can of course be powerful, as at Pentecost when it gave birth to the church, but it is also so perilous that Jesus instructed us to do it privately, as we shall appreciate in chapter thirteen.

The Reverend Doctor Herb Barks, now president of Baylor School in Chattanooga, Tennessee, confessed to learning this lesson after his first year at seminary. He returned home and a friend invited him to lunch in a large urban restaurant. Herb was feeling that he had absorbed as much about God as anyone who had ever lived.

As soon as they had been served, Herb self-righteously suggested, "Don't you think we ought to thank God before we, uh, eat?" His friend was equal to the occasion and solemnly responded, "Of course." The friend then rose, picked up his teaspoon and tapped a water glass until the large dining room was hushed. Then he announced in a devastating voice, "Mr. Herbert Barks of Columbia Seminary in Atlanta has asked to return thanks." Herb never prayed for a long time after that till he had carefully shut the door.

What has happened to public worship is something like what we have done with the restaurant routine of "Happy Birthday to You." The waiters gather 'round the victim, who is sitting there with that not-too-generous chunk of white plaster plunked in front of him with a sputtering candle punched into it. Then comes the dreary rendering of "Happy Birthday," which can be the unhappiest song, particularly as rendered ad infinitum by the subsidized glee club. Here it's your birthday, and they are putting you through the same lifeless jingle they put everyone else through, and there's no way you can get out of it. You would be a spoilsport to refuse it.

The entire scene is a dreary replica of the rituals we subject ourselves to in so many church services, very reminiscent of the way we've commercialized the original Lord's Supper.

Think of God, His birthdays going by, sitting at His table, miserable from these everlasting ditties.

Just because we've sung happy birthday to God loudly doesn't mean we've praised Him. Jack Benny made fun of such monkey business with his violin. When the audience started to leave, he followed them still sawing away on his Strad, which was no Stradivarius, but made by Joe Strad.

God is sick and tired of having pet phrases pawned off on Him. God blew up over such repetitious mediocrity.

To what purpose is the multitude of your sacrifices unto me? saith the Lord: I am full of the burnt offerings of rams, and the fat of fed beasts; And I delight not in the blood of bullocks, or of lambs, or of he goats. . . . Bring no more vain oblations; incense is an abomination unto me; the new moons and sabbaths, the calling of assemblies, I cannot away with [endure]

... even the solemn meeting. Your new moons and your ap-
pointed feasts, my soul hateth: they are a trouble unto me; I
am weary to bear them.

Isaiah 1:11–14

We cannot shrug off Jesus' withering words to the hypocrites; He may be talking to us. And He had more suggestions
than silent prayers. ..."Hypocrites! You travel over sea and
land to win one convert; and when you have won him you
make him twice as fit for hell as you are yourselves" (Matthew
23:15 NEB). Jesus abhorred such practices as grabbing the best
seats, showing off with long prayers, having faith like mountains, and moving mustard seeds into the sea.

Anyone who dares to say good things about God better
watch out. Jesus rejected one woman's compliments: "Blessed
is the womb that bare thee, and the paps which thou hast
sucked. But he said, Yea rather, blessed are they that hear the
word of God, and keep it" (Luke 11:27–28).

Many of Jesus' comments are warnings about church services and church people. "And he spake this parable unto certain which trusted in themselves that they were righteous, and
despised others" (Luke 18:9).

It is a misunderstanding to think that God craves a perpetual
eulogy of banal letters, as though He would like nothing better
than for someone to whip out a song and sling it at Him. And
unless we come through with something at least every seven
days, we're in for it, as the Psalmist seems to suggest—as
though God lived on compliments.

We don't praise our favorite quarterback because it will
make him feel good. We are on our feet roaring approbation
because of his performance. He wins it from us by his yardage.

So we truly praise God, not because we'd better, but because
of His record. There's never been another like Him. We build
up our gridiron hero with his statistics: the year he won

the Heisman trophy and was all-American. We appreciate God the same way, citing His spectacular splitting of the Red Sea that engineered Moses' impressive prison break.

Just as our running back wins his stardom by specific accomplishments, so it is with God. We do not appreciate a God in general. We never really get excited about God until we "count His blessings, one by one." Only then, as the words go in the old hymn, will it "surprise you what the Lord hath done."

More important, God not only received His glory through specific accomplishments: "You will find a babe lying in a manger"; "There was a shout from the center cross . . . the sky went black . . . and the earth shook." Beyond these grand gestures is the further specific that these actions were done especially for each of us.

A little boy with leukemia in a hospital in New York not only received a card from the team saying that they were playing to win for him, his favorite sports hero personally visited him. That is what does it in Christianity. "Jesus did this for you and me." "He came to me that unforgettable time." "O happy day," I'll have to sing about that, or give the rebel yell, or "Rally 'round the flag, boys, rally once again." "And the huge stone was slammed back." This will take a shout from the housetops from all of us.

The fans at the Rose Bowl were on their feet yelling, not simply to crank up their stars on the field; the stars cranked them up. And so our praise to God is the overwhelming admiration and thanks we cannot hold back in response to getting our voice back, being able to see again, getting that phone call, or falling in love.

C. S. Lewis proves that praise pours from our enjoyment in the same way as the sports fan is aroused by his hero. We make an awful mistake when we make worship a chore or a guilt trip, or a way to win points. The true worshiper is someone who flies to the front pew fresh from a miracle.

Better yet, before he flew to that front pew perhaps he did something like Chief Dan George's father. Dan George recalled: "I remember as a little boy, fishing with him up Indian River and I can still see him as the sun rose above the mountain top in the early morning . . . I can see him standing by the water's edge with his arms raised above his head while he softly moaned . . . 'Thank You, Thank You.' It left a deep impression on my young mind" (*My Heart Soars*, Hancock House, 1974).

And when we praise someone, really enjoy them that much, we must show and tell. I never heard of a genuine sports fan who was not evangelical. If we loved our vacation spot, or the sausage they served, or the four-wheel drive, or Bach's *B Minor Mass,* we'll soon be on the phone soliciting converts.

So with God. If He's any good to us, we won't be able to keep Him to ourselves. Let's hope we'll evangelize in better taste than pulling lapels and putting up signs. But even without our saying anything, any enjoyment of God bestows presence on the participants. The shout from the housetops can come through the pores and emanate from the sparkle in the eyes. Our joy evokes responses in others, simply by where we're coming from and going to.

THE BEST NEED YOU MOST

We remember, Lord,
The black thoughts you banished
From the Head of Legion, and
The bent back you straightened
For that poor woman
That morning in the synagogue.
It all comes back to us now
In the Book where it is written down;
The heavy load of care you lifted
From the bowed shoulders of Mary,
The pride you melted in
The heart of Nicodemus,
The agony that you healed
In the heart of hated Zacchaeus,
To say nothing of the blind terror
You quickly dismissed
In the thief beside you
As you yourself hung over
The hole of death.

Knowing that you showed them
No favoritism you would deny us,
We wait our turn
Praying for forgiveness
For our impatience
And lack of faith.

7

The Bible's Prayerbook

Every people produces its popular music from what it worries about, what it wants. Ancient Britain cut her teeth on never-ending epics like *Beowulf,* then got down to little ballads like "Get Up and Bar the Door." Chanteys went to sea with the bosun's pipe, and minstrels went into castles to set King Arthur's days to strings. America's folk music came out of the Wild West, down from the mountains, and up from the Old South. It has gone from "Yankee Doodle" to hard rock.

There was once a people whose hit tunes were anthems, and all their music was meant for God. They did not sing about "My Old Kentucky Home," but about Zion; and their Stephen Foster was a soldier-saint. It became second nature for them to sing the praises of the living God. He was their hero and all their tall tales were saved up for Him. Their Moses would not take the credit. Their King David stepped down so the people could see the Power behind the throne. He was the first to say that he did not slay Goliath singlehandedly, and the band that danced him into Jerusalem played sacred music.

We have gone through jingles very fast: jazz, blues, spirituals, and gospel songs—none very spiritual. But there was another day when prayer was the music men wanted to hear and psalms were the songs they loved to sing. Their harp still shames our saxophone. We have not been able to do better and so we go back to them now.

The psalms are not psalms—precisely. The Latin *psalmi* came from the Greek Septuagint, *psalmoi,* denoting a striking or twitching with the fingers. The word in the Hebrew text is *tephillim,* which Israel had taken to mean "praises" or "songs of praise." The first name given to the psalms was "prayers" (*tephilloth*), and the word "praises," or "psalms," was coined from their musical accompaniment. While they were set to music and have been sung and chanted in church and temple ever since, they were prayed first. The Book of Psalms, in the beginning and deep down, was not a congregational hymnal, but a book made of many books of private prayers.

Scholars are still scuffling over the age of these prayers and who wrote them. Robert H. Pfeiffer feels they are too modern for David, and that they must have been brought back from the Exile and benefited from the insights of the later prophets. He believes they are no more than two or three centuries older than Christ. But if that were true, Christ and His contemporaries could not have been so confident of David's touch in the psalms.

No doubt the Book of Psalms was the work of many ages of hours and a chorus of folded hands, for we know now, from excavation and research, that not all of God's good ideas burst upon mankind in the last few minutes before the birth of Christ. History's most precious thoughts were not neatly stored up for us in one particular place in time, but were scattered indiscriminately through life's pages. The song of Miriam, in Exodus 15:21, is written in the style of a psalm and is thought to be from the time of Moses. The Exile forged as many psalms from sorrow as from the inspiration of Jeremiah, but there are many clues leading us to the traditional conviction that earlier psalmists cheered the later prophets just as that "sweet psalmist" revived King Saul.

We cannot believe Scripture stamped David's name so indelibly upon the psalms simply to give them royal standing.

They bear his name, we believe, because they look much like him. They reflect the rich mixture of his personality—sweet shepherd and beloved king with feet of clay and heart of gold, barbarian and saint, a man among men at war and in prayer. The psalms introduce a man who had compressed into his own nature and into his prayers "all the emotions," as John Calvin claims, "of which anyone can be conscious." The old intellectual who wrote Ecclesiasticus was not easily fooled. He saw through all the times and turns it took to put down these old prayers in black and white; he saw far enough through David's failings to find him at his prayers; and then he did an unforgettable thing. He pinned this note to David: "In all his works he praised . . . with his whole heart. . . ."

And David, in one word, defines the psalms. He is not Moses or Elijah. He is one of us. Perhaps David gets more blame or credit than he deserves, but the name David is one way of describing what we see in these devotions that still appeal to us so powerfully after thousands of years. They are so human; running in one short sentence from the ridiculously savage to the sublime. They are brutally fresh, frank, childlike, and at times childish. The ferocity and faith of man are bared before God. They are not the typical words the cynic likes to put in the mouth of his porcelain saint. They are prayers for adults only and for children only—only for those who are honest enough to admit to guilt and good enough to invite God. The psalms are the virile explosions of a chastened soldier, combat softened by heartbreak and exaltation, someone who needs God to talk to, to appreciate and understand him, and to give him a little more help right away.

The psalms belong to someone besides David, for in another sense they are the psalms of Christ, who quoted from them more than any other book. Along with all the prayers He taught the disciples, these old psalms were on His lips, word for word, in times of temptation, in Gethsemane, and while He hung on a cross. Christians come to the psalms indirectly through Christ because they meant so much to Him and because they must be read in His light. We want to know what the psalmist meant when he wrote them, but ultimately we want to know the meaning Christ gave to them.

There is more to the psalms than they could see at first, until Someone took them seriously and went beyond them. Christ did not change them; He carried them out, giving them a confirmation that their first readers could not give. And we are pilgrims, not scholars; we want to know what God, not His ghostwriters, had in mind. It is because Christ found the psalms, loved them, used them and finished them, that "no other book with the exception perhaps of the Gospels and some of Paul's letters has gone," as Stewart McCullough writes, "so directly to the heart of Christendom."

Something terrible has happened to the psalms in the modern mind. It has lost them, one after another, until most of us are down to two in memory: The Twenty-third and Old Hundredth. Our fathers knew all the psalms almost as well as Jesus did. Paul and Silas chanted psalms at midnight in their prison cell in Philippi. Christians, condemned to die, entered the Roman arenas singing, "I will bless the Lord at all times; His praise shall continually be in my mouth." W. O. E. Oesterly tells us: "St. Gennadius, Patriarch of Constantinople, would not ordain any clerk who could not recite the whole psalter. St. Gregory refused to consecrate a Bishop for the same reason. The eighth council of Toledo (A.D. 653) orders that none henceforth shall be promoted to any ecclesiastical dignity who do not know the whole psalter. St. Patrick, we are told, recited the psalter daily, and St. Kentigen did the same every night."

Samuel Terrien reminds us how practical and busy the psalms have been in bravery. The gallant reformer John Huss stepped up to his stake to be burned in 1415 reciting Psalm 31; Sir Thomas More waited for his execution with some lines from Psalm 51; and Martin Luther's famous hymn, "A Mighty Fortress Is Our God," was inspired by Psalm 46. The pilgrims sang psalms on the Mayflower, "and it was after a verse of Psalm 76, 'at Salem is his tabernacle,' that pioneers named the first settlement of the Massachusetts Bay Colony. The Bay Psalm Book was the third volume ever published in America."

When our tiny country was turning blue in stillbirth at the Constitutional Convention in 1789, Benjamin Franklin broke the deadlock with a moving reminder from Psalm 127: "Except the Lord build the house, they labour in vain that build it . . . ." Lincoln might have found "Fourscore," for the beginning of his Gettysburg Address, in the tenth verse of Psalm 90; and in one of the most eloquent moments of American literature, his Second Inaugural Address, he introduced the memorable passage, "with malice toward none," with these words from Psalm 19: ". . . the judgments of the Lord are true and righteous altogether."

Memorization does not go far enough and it can miss the meaning of words, yet we know that the mind has to hold something close for a long time to love it—to do it. We remember dates important to us—our birthdays, paydays, words, and numbers that we want to remember—and tend to forget whatever we don't want to do. Why don't we return to this treasury of prayers at the heart of the Bible until they belong to their rightful owners once again? They can do something wonderful for us and to us, as they did for that prodigal son Augustine, when they made him cry in his *Confessions:* "O in what accents spake I unto Thee, my God, when I read the Psalms of David . . . How was I by them kindled toward Thee."

AN ALL-PURPOSE PRAYER

Some of us are searching
For the right word,
Like the Centurion who asked: "Lord,
Only say the word, and
My servant shall be healed."
Others are lost and
Need only a gesture from you
As Philip did:
"Lord, show us the way."
Some of us are still struggling
With prehistoric monsters
Like resentment. And we
Bite our lips because
We have to go back and ask you once more
So dumb a question as Peter
Blurted out: "Lord,
How often can my brother offend me,
And I still forgive him?"
Finally, there are those beside us
Who do not have the heart
For any more questions.
They don't even know what to ask
And pray blindly
Through their tears
Simply for you to sit beside them
As you did John that night.
And if there is anyone
Who could not bear that much light
Would you please nod to them, or
Glance their way, or remember them,
Lord, as you promised you would the thief,
"When you come into your Kingdom"?

8

The Twenty-third Psalm

The Lord is my shepherd; I shall not want.
He maketh me to lie down in green pastures:
He leadeth me beside the still waters.
He restoreth my soul:
He leadeth me in the paths of righteousness
       for his name's sake.
Yea, though I walk
       through the valley of the shadow of death,
I will fear no evil: for thou art with me;
Thy rod and thy staff they comfort me.
Thou preparest a table
       before me in the presence of mine enemies:
Thou anointest my head with oil; my cup
       runneth over.
Surely goodness and mercy
       shall follow me all the days of my life:
And I will dwell
       in the house of the Lord for ever.

Those psalms our fathers learned to pray as children, kept by heart for life, and whispered last, are lost to us. We rack our brains in vain for some shred of the Scriptures that meant far more to them than we could say. The commandments are no longer at our command, commanding us. Who can make them add up to ten? Today's Bibles, with their pages still stuck together, do not open by themselves to familiar, well-thumbed places. The lordly language of a once magnificent tradition has fallen in ruins at the feet of our forgetfulness.

One little prayer stands untouched by time, not yet dropped and broken by busy hands that can't be still and don't have time. It is still in use and it has a way with our latest fears. It was left behind by a shepherd boy near the beginning of the Book, as that Good Shepherd left His prayer near the end. It has no name, only a number.

"The Lord is my shepherd."   Could not everyone say yes to that? No. We slip over it so easily we do not realize how much it is saying. This is not the least the Old Testament says, it is the most. If a man waters down his faith, this is the first to go. Anyone who believes that God is his Shepherd believes the almost unbelievable. Today a man might say that if God is Shepherd, He must be cruel or incompetent, for mankind looks like sheep without a shepherd. Who was watching over the little lambs at Hiroshima, Auschwitz, Andersonville, or our horror of "the day after"? Cancer and head-on collisions severely challenge God's credentials, and there is enough sorrow in the most successful life to arouse suspicion in His Shepherdhood.

Where can one see God working as Shepherd in the space age? He isn't dressed that way in the book of the month, or in the college religion course. Tennessee Williams could see hell very well and was about to call God off. But that is nothing new. History is jammed with the same old complaints and curses. The news is that someone's voice once rose reverently above the raving horde to say: "The Lord is my shepherd."

David did more than sing these words for Saul. It was not an easy age then. He took them into battle with him against Goliath, for he took no confidence in, nor credit for, his sling and stones. His answer to the giant's taunt had this higher ring:

"You come to me with a sword. . . but I come to you in the name of the Lord of hosts . . ." (*see* 1 Samuel 17:45). What a foolish lad, the Philistines figured. But David won and the words of the psalm brought him something sweeter than victory, as they have to many others time after time. Men have been able to stand up to the fury of the storm by saying them; they come back singing them, somehow satisfied even in defeat and death.

Catching God in a shepherd's clothing takes more than a quick mind. It is a matter of one's will being broken before God. It is something the "man from Missouri" will never be shown, nor the antagonistic sophomore. Divinity does not cater to the cynic or trot to the bleat of adolescent defiance. A shepherd becomes real, as any sheep knows, only under the drastic terms of "unconditional surrender." The psalmist found this shining faith by trial and error. He ran into it in his daily activities. Is the Lord my Shepherd? Only one way to find out. Obey.

"I shall not want." At first that sounds like a racket of words or a paradise for fools. If we take this psalm seriously, God must be doing much more work than we ever dreamed. If "The Lord is my shepherd," then we have a security that laughs at our strongboxes. It also puts life under an altogether different light and power. It means that here on earth God is the perfect Host, and perhaps we've not been behaving well as guests. Men can make themselves believe that they are bringing home the bacon or that they have found their green pastures all by themselves. Our instinct for self-preservation may become abnormally swollen. We ridicule the sloppy businessman who doesn't know where his next nickel is coming from, but do *we* know? We have grazed off the fat of the land, by the fat of our intellect and the fat of our opportunity, and then we have the nerve to congratulate ourselves. We can't see

how the sparrows deserve any applause for their prosperity, yet somehow in the quirk of the ego we feel we should take a bow for ours.

The Twenty-third Psalm does not cancel pension plans, but it puts them in their place and takes the note of desperation out of the insurance policy. It does not encourage carelessness, but it challenges faith and offers a new interpretation in which we find that every bit of help we get is another way His shepherd's crook will work. Will God do less for us than for lilies? Man has more, and so he needs more, because he has many more miles to go. "Consider the ravens: they neither sow nor reap, they have neither storehouse nor barn, and yet God feeds them. Of how much more value are you than the birds!" (Luke 12:24 RSV). The psalmist had the honesty and the height to have the happy thought that God is why he would not want, and God it is who "*. . . maketh me to lie down in green pastures . . . .*"

"*. . . leadeth me beside the still waters. He restoreth my soul . . . .*" Our day is like a child constantly in motion, every minute crammed so tight that we must drive faster. The unforgivable sin is to not be busy. But the Bible insists that life's biggest thrills take place not when a man is in the air going somewhere, but when he is actually sitting still. The big day ahead of us is not the trip to the moon or meeting another planet's men, but our trip to meet God the Father Almighty. And a blind man may arrive there by rocking chair.

This psalm is a reorientation from what man does to what God does. The things worth mentioning in a man's life may not be the distinguished activities listed in his résumé, but the day he was born—not a "Do-it-yourself" project. Time grows precious to a man not when he is speeding, speaking, or on the road, but when he gives birth to a good idea. Surely Moses, for all his mighty string of "firsts," if asked about his finest hours, would not remember what he had done but what had happened to him—a burning bush, the day he stood by the Red Sea and saw in breathless awe the salvation of the Lord.

Our day may need not more organizations and activities, but more rest. Men not only get run down, but they run out of faith. No matter how old and wise they grow they still mill about like sheep and do not know when to go to bed or get down on their knees. They can't seem to relax without a "little something." Could man need shepherding as well as drugs? The psalmist testified, "He maketh me to lie down . . ." Man needs a drink of something stronger than alcohol to keep his spirits up. ". . . he leadeth me beside the still waters," the psalmist said. It is not enough to be saved all over again at every revival. Man needs a daily ration of manna, of the blessings that must be imported daily, only from heaven, by prayer. "He restoreth my soul . . . ."

". . . he leadeth me . . ." The phrase is easily said, but the idea is almost dead to the world. It does not get into the official publicity on personnel and guidance, or in the news. What reputable vocational counselor would dare bring up God's will in his interviews? The psychiatrist will approve it only from the patient's point of view, as a possible "pill." The very idea has become embarrassing, poor taste in polished circles, except for the most formal ceremonies. It's excusable, of course, in clergymen. Prayers open the lips in Congress, but the ears may be at the polls. We excuse ourselves by mumbling something about being practical; how can a man stay in business, or in office, if he operates in the psalmist's way? Who leads you and me?

Could providence be true instead of coincidental? Could it be that the Bible is not bluffing? Could God be a Guide, with His finger crooked at each of us? Do you suppose that before the creation of His big business He did some careful, long-range planning, in detail? Did He make each man with something special in mind? Might He have a reason for each talent

He hands out? Did He send His only Son in the hope that we too would be His sons, go into business with Him, take that opening He has for us? Is God merely a hands-off grandfatherly figure, feebly saying no from the sidelines? An impersonal, futile, cosmic force? Or is He Someone who watches over us, comforts and commands us?

"Yea, though I walk through the valley of the shadow of death, I will fear no evil: for thou art with me...." The psalmist does not say he is not afraid. But these "dark shadows" do not make him die a thousand deaths. Dying is bigger than going down to the barber shop, but "I will fear no evil...." The key to our last errand is not a pocketful of grit saved up, but a strategic friendship made while the sun was still shining. In the darkness when I cannot see, *"... thy rod and thy staff they comfort me."* God is not a strange prosecutor waiting for us in a foreign court, but the familiar Counsel for our defense, proven by "the still waters."

"Thou preparest a table before me in the presence of mine enemies...." God is different—He is not made the way man has made Him. He is too good to be accounted for or predicted. He puts on His biggest banquet for us, not when things are running like clockwork but when things go wrong. Men take it for granted that if disaster strikes, God must be out of the picture, but faith works best in a crisis. God originated and perfected the element of surprise. It is in the middle of catastrophe that God sends in the neighbors and the table groans with goodness. If we do not lose our heads, God can best be seen when the bottom seems to be falling out of life.

Heaven comes in the same breath as death. The grave was where the resurrection came. The ungodly man comes out, after the explosion, choked up with profanity, renewing his mutiny against religion. But Peter and John, after that last turn of the screw, stumbled blindly about, not from heartbreak but from the power and the glory. The pagan calls tragedy a dirty trick; the scream is chronic: "What is there to live for now?" But a modern Job, floored by calamity, is the first to rise to his feet to speak of the tender, loving care of God. Faith finds a blessing in the ashes of despair and sees in the distance, beyond the smoking ruins, the rising spires of another city. "Thou preparest a table before me in the presence of mine enemies. . . ." It may not be until a man is down and hears the count of nine that he will ever know enough to say, *"My cup runneth over."*

"Surely goodness and mercy shall follow me all the days of my life. . . ." Luck changes, economy fluctuates, but the love of God holds steady. Past kindness is a promise that there is more to come and the psalmist did not dread the days ahead. It seemed to him that he would never be completely on his own, or thrown away, no matter what age and sin might do to him. Later on, someone with better eyes would look down that same street and notice God leaving the ninety-nine to save the blackest sheep. A man cannot be sure that he will stay good forever, but he can steady himself with the thought that throughout all his "length of days, thy goodness faileth never."

". . . and I will dwell in the house of the Lord . . . ." Literally, the Hebrew may be translated: "as long as I live," but as we can see by Christian light, and in the light of all the psalmist said, it is as King James's men were inspired to say, *"for ever."* The God of the universe did not intend to preside over a cosmic suicide. He is not the caretaker of a mushrooming cemetery, but the Father of the world of the living. He was not unfairly prejudiced against poor people who lived short lives of misery in the past, nor is He planning to make immortal pets of some future breed of supermen. Man will have to go far to mean more to Him than His Son—or any man who ever fell among thieves. Our God is "the God of Abraham, and the God of Isaac." Your God.

This Twenty-third prayer introduces a God who does not say, "I'll love you till you're twelve, or you're on your own, or get sick, or senile." He loves you. He loves old grandma as much as any new grandson. The kind of love we learn about in this old masterpiece of prayer is the love that finishes strong with "forever."

WERE YOU THERE?

Lord, I can handle losers
Like a good Samaritan.
I'm tough with those who've had it
Hard and need my help.
But when someone comes along
Who is better than I am,
Better off,
I fall apart.
Anyone whose prayers have been answered
Turns me off.
Then the urge to kill comes out
In me. You can tell
By the way I make those cracks.
Of course I'd never
Kill them in one blow;
Just a little nibble at a time.
I only mean to give their ears a trim.
They say Jesus suffered three hours.
My victims suffer longer.
It's like a living death I give them
With my glances of disapproval.
Those people know I don't like them.
Some of them don't even exist for me.
If looks could kill,
If thoughts can throw
Prayer in reverse,
And the devil's quick to answer
My worst wishes toward those
Who show me up,
Who could better understand than I
The mob that shouted "Crucify"

Good Friday. That's exactly where I am.
Thirsty for the blood of anybody
Who's better than I am.
"Sometimes it causes me to tremble."

9

Samplings from Unexpected Quarters

Mark Twain has been unjustly stereotyped as an unbeliever. Most people profess more belief than they have; Mark Twain had far more faith than he professed. Any reader of his autobiography must be struck by the unequaled spirit of thanksgiving he possessed at the close of his hard life.

I offer this passage as an illustration of how mistaken we are to rule out prayer in someone's life because of brash statements, or because of a stern antipathy to self-righteousness, such as Twain had. Perhaps this chapter will act as a check on our proclivity to write people off who don't parrot our religious phrases according to our party line. Many Christians, and Christian deeds, are hidden by our blind side. Often we don't see Jesus in others because of our own immodesty or prejudice, but one can't miss seeing God in Twain here:

As I have said, I spent some part of every year at the farm until I was twelve or thirteen years old. The life which I led there with my cousins was full of charm, and so is the memory of it yet. I can call back the solemn twilight and mystery of the deep woods, the earthy smells, the faint odors of the wild flowers, the sheen of rain-washed foliage, the rattling clatter of drops when the wind shook the trees, the far-off hammering of woodpeckers and the muffled drumming of wood pheasants in the remoteness of the forest, the snapshot glimpses of disturbed wild creatures scurrying through the grass—I can call it all back and make it as real as it ever was, and as blessed.

I can call back the prairie, and its loneliness and peace, and a vast hawk hanging motionless in the sky, with his wings spread wide and the blue of the vault showing through the fringe of their end feathers. I can see the woods in their autumn dress, the oaks purple, the hickories washed with gold, the maples and the sumachs luminous with crimson fires, and I can hear the rustle made by the fallen leaves as we plowed through them. I can see the blue clusters of wild grapes hanging among the foliage of the saplings, and I remember the taste of them and the smell. I know how the wild blackberries looked, and how they tasted, and the same with the pawpaws, the hazelnuts, and the persimmons; and I can feel the thumping rain, upon my head, of hickory nuts and walnuts when we were out in the frosty dawn to scramble for them with the pigs, and the gusts of wind loosed them and sent them down.

I know the stain of blackberries, and how pretty it is, and I know the stain of walnut hulls, and how little it minds soap and water, also what grudged experience it had of either of them. I know the taste of maple sap, and when to gather it, and how to arrange the troughs and the delivery tubes, and how to boil down the juice, and how to hook the sugar after it is made, also how much better hooked sugar tastes than any that is honestly come by, let bigots say what they will. I know how a prize watermelon looks when it is sunning its fat rotundity among pumpkin vines and "simblins"; I know how to tell when it is ripe without "plugging" it; I know how inviting it looks when it is cooling itself in a tub of water under the bed, waiting; I know how it looks when it lies on the table in the sheltered great floor space between house and kitchen, and the children gathered for the sacrifice and their mouths watering;

I know the crackling sound it makes when the carving knife enters its end, and I can see the split fly along in front of the blade as the knife cleaves its way to the other end; I can see its halves fall apart and display the rich red meat and the black seeds, and the heart standing up, a luxury fit for the elect; I know how a boy looks behind a yard-long slice of that melon, and I know how he feels; for I have been there. I know the taste of the watermelon which has been honestly come by, and I know the taste of the watermelon which has been acquired by art. Both taste good, but the experienced know which tastes best.

I know the look of green apples and peaches and pears on the trees, and I know how entertaining they are when they are inside of a person. I know how ripe ones look when they are piled in pyramids under the trees, and how pretty they are and how vivid their colors. I know how a frozen apple looks, in a barrel down cellar in the wintertime, and how hard it is to bite, and how the frost makes the teeth ache, and yet how good it is, notwithstanding. I know the disposition of elderly people to select the specked apples for the children, and I once knew ways to beat the game. I know the look of an apple that is roasting and sizzling on a hearth on a winter's evening, and I know the comfort that comes of eating it hot, along with some sugar and a drench of cream. I know the delicate art and mystery of so cracking hickory nuts and walnuts on a flatiron with a hammer that the kernels will be delivered whole, and I know how the nuts, taken in conjunction with winter apples, cider, and doughnuts, make old people's old tales and old jokes sound fresh and crisp and enchanting, and juggle an evening away before you know what went with the time. I know the look of Uncle Dan'l's kitchen as it was on the privileged nights, when I was a child, and I can see the white and black children grouped on the hearth, with firelight playing on their faces and the shadows flickering upon the walls, clear back toward the cavernous gloom of the rear, and I can hear Uncle Dan'l telling the immortal tales which Uncle Remus Harris was to gather into his book and charm the world with, by and by; and I can feel again the creepy joy which quivered through me when the time for the ghost story was reached— and the sense of regret, too, which came over me, for it was always the last story of the evening and there was nothing between it and the unwelcomed bed.

I can remember the bare wooden stairway in my uncle's house, and the turn to the left above the landing, and the rafters and the slanting roof over my bed, and the squares of moonlight on the floor, and the white cold world of snow outside, seen through the curtainless window. I can remember the howling of the wind and the quaking of the house on stormy nights, and how snug and cozy one felt, under the blankets, listening; and how the powdery snow used to sift in, around the sashes, and lie in little ridges on the floor and make the place look chilly in the morning and curb the wild desire to get up—in case there was any. I can remember how very dark that room was, in the dark of the moon, and how packed it was with ghostly stillness when one woke up by accident away in the night, and forgotten sins came flocking out of the secret chambers of the memory and wanted a hearing; and how ill-chosen the time seemed for this kind of business; and how dismal was the hoo-hooing of the owl and the wailing of the wolf, sent mourning by on the night wind.

I remember the raging of the rain on that roof, summer nights, and how pleasant it was to lie and listen to it, and enjoy the white splendor of the lightning and the majestic booming and crashing of the thunder. It was a very satisfactory room, and there was a lightning rod which was reachable from the window, an adorable and skittish thing to climb up

and down, summer nights, when there were duties on hand of
a sort to make privacy desirable. . . .

I remember the squirrel hunts, and prairie-chicken hunts,
and wild-turkey hunts, and all that; and how we turned out,
mornings, while it was still dark, to go on these expeditions,
and how chilly and dismal it was, and how often I regretted
that I was well enough to go. A toot on a tin horn brought
twice as many dogs as were needed, and in their happiness
they raced and scampered about, and knocked small people
down, and made no end of unnecessary noise. At the word,
they vanished away toward the woods, and we drifted silently
after them in the melancholy gloom. But presently the gray
dawn stole over the world, the birds piped up, then the sun
rose and poured light and comfort all around, everything was
fresh and dewy and fragrant, and life was a boon again. After
three hours of tramping we arrived back wholesomely tired,
overladen with game, very hungry, and just in time for break-
fast.

And if Twain's praise surprises you, is it not unusual that a
great Christian of modern times, Aleksandr Solzhenitsyn,
emerged from the shadows of the Kremlin without the assis-
tance of a missionary from the West?

I remember how astounded I was to learn of the conversion
of Stalin's daughter Svetlana a few years ago, but Solzhenitsyn's conversion was a greater miracle because of the subse-
quent impact his writings have been having on the world.
Apparently God commissioned him to tell the truth about the
crimes of the Communists, on behalf of the sixty to one hundred million Russians who died in the Gulag Archipelago. No
one can miss this amazing witness in his most recent autobio-
graphical volume, *The Oak and the Calf.* He reports that the
Communist founders believed their political program to be ab-

solutely impregnable. And Solzhenitsyn says that they thought
of everything except one thing—a miracle. It is becoming ever
so clear that Solzhenitsyn is a huge instrument in that miracle.
God knows where it will end.

One of the first pieces of Solzhenitsyn's praise to come to the
West was a prayer my wife discovered in *Vogue* magazine. It
had found its way past the censor by samizat, which is the
hand-copying method Russians use to publish and circulate
underground. Much of the drama of that prayer lies in the circumstances out of which it came. He had been in prison and in
labor camps for eight years. His father had died when he was a
child. During his imprisonment his mother died and his wife
divorced him; he contracted a cancer which was growing in his
abdomen so rapidly he could tell each evening that it had
grown since morning. It was then, in the blackness of that
hour, that this prayer came to him.

> How simple for me to live with you, O Lord
> How easy to believe in you
> When in confusion my soul bares itself or bends,
> When the most wise can see
> No further than this night and do not know
> What the morrow brings.
>
> You fill me with the clear certainty
> That You exist and that You watch
> To see that all the paths
> Of righteousness be not closed.
>
> From the heights of worldly glory
> I am astonished by the path
> Through despair you have provided me—
> This path from which I have been
> Worthy enough to reflect Your radiance to man.

> All that I will
> yet reflect, You will grant me
> And for that which I will
> not succeed in reflecting
> You have appointed others.

And finally Solzhenitsyn's tiny psalm from "The Prison Chronicle":

> Live with a steady superiority over life—don't be afraid of misfortune, and do not yearn after happiness. It is, after all, all the same. The bitter doesn't last forever, and the sweet never fills the cup to overflowing. It is enough if you don't freeze in the cold and if hunger and thirst don't claw at your sides.
>
> If your back isn't broken, if your feet can walk, if both arms work, if both eyes can see, and if both ears can hear, then whom should you envy? And why? Our envy of others devours us most of all. Rub your eyes and purify your heart and prize above all else in the world those who love you and those you wish well.
>
> Do not hurt them or scold them, and never part from any of them in anger—after all you simply do not know: It might be your *last* act before your arrest and that will be how you are imprinted in their memory.

Prayer comes not only from suspects like Mark Twain, and illegally from behind the Iron Curtain. Our most genuinely moving prayers have often come from someone whom our pride may have dismissed as a dirty old man, when God knows he's a dirty old angel.

Hondo Crouch was called "The Clown Prince of Texas." He dressed like a prospector who never found gold. He was a lovable old rascal who ran around with his guitar and Mexican songs, looking for a beer. He found that the town of Luckenbach, Texas, was for sale. It consisted of two or three half-deserted houses and a post office/beer joint. It hit the right spot on his way home from work, so he bought it.

Hondo immediately made himself prime minister and seceded from the Union. He put up a parking meter, and put in air mail service by nailing a mailbox to the top of a twenty-foot pole. He improved the municipal park by taking down the old rubber tire swing and replacing it with a whitewall tire.

Hondo held chili cook-offs and even the Luckenbach World's Fair to which ten thousand people came. He fired antique cannons and passed out purple hearts to the people who fell down best. He achieved enough notoriety to attract visitors such as Festus from television's "Gunsmoke." When they met, Festus said, "You must be Hondo." "Yup, you must be Festus." "Yup." Then Hondo added, "Are you as disappointed as I am?"

Hondo began public life as an Olympic swimmer and ended as an actor, playing the part of a preacher conducting a funeral in a 1975 film entitled, *The Last Pony Express.* At the cast party, Hondo was given the coffin used in the film. Hondo hauled it everywhere in the back of his pickup. When someone would ask about it, he would answer, "I may go anytime." He did go shortly after that, and his daughter, Becky Patterson, took his cremated remains, which had been wrapped in a red bandanna for the service at the Episcopal Church in Fredricksburg, Texas, and scattered them at his favorite gopher hole, his laughing place, and the secluded thicket where he had found the fawn for her.

I am indebted to Becky for my Hondo material. She has become a distinguished artist and author. Her *Hondo, My Father* (Shoalcreek Press) is a little masterpiece, for she has been able not only to appreciate the prophetic role of jester, which Hondo came very nearly achieving nationally, but also has caught her father at "Daybreak," which is what Hondo called the piece which concludes this chapter:

Nothin' much happened last month at Luckenbach, 'cept the potato chip man came by—forgot about that; O, then there was daylight. A Luckenbach daylight is that time of day you wish would never go 'way, when bang—all o' sudden there's no dark and there's no light and it's foggy and it isn't. It's as humble as a life bein' born. Ain't that nearly a blessing? Daylight on earth is when light is busy makin' lil' ole nothing's into somethin's. And sometimes big brown bears turn into just big brown rocks.

Daylight in the winter is when little dripping icicles get a new hold on their host and Jack Frost is busy rollin' up his carpet, always from east to west, that covers the hills we love so.

Daylight in the spring is when little dewdrops are just clinging onto grass tips, just shiverin' from fright in the early morning light, 'cause they know the sun is fixing to love 'em to death. Don't know why they shiver—happens every morning. I guess they have hope.

Daylight in summer is when lil' old ladies are thinking about puttin' on big ole bonnets and long sleeves to hide from the sun, and lil' young ladies are thinkin' 'bout takin' off all their clothes to lie in it—scares me. And mama's thinkin' 'bout pullin' the shades in the living room, where no one has ever really lived, so the sun won't sadden the colors of the rug.

Daylight in the fall is when big-eyed deer are gettin' closer to the ground. They know that this time of day red-eyed hunters with heavy rifles will soon be stumbling thru the brush again—and again and again. Big trees brace themselves—the first norther's gonna tug pretty colors out of jes' plain leaves—then walk off.

A Luckenbach daylight really is that time when there's just thousands and thousands of insignificant miracles happenin'—little quiet nightfeeders softly rememberin' their way home and soon their little delicate night tracks will be erased by big fussy day ones, and the squawkin' mockingbird will wake the sun and the sun will tell the mama hoot owl it's time to fuss her big-eyed babies to bed. And all the stars that were admired last night will take a back seat in the bus, and the fantastic firefly will be just a bug; but a giant weed will turn into a beautiful sunflower. Then there's that unbelievable smell of fresh coffee and leathery ranchers sittin' around sippin' too many cups, just to keep from going to work, until the distant instant naggin' of a chain saw jerks 'em back into reality. Little empty lunch pails are meetin' full ones on the freeway.

You know, my music makin' friends never get to enjoy all this purty stuff. They're too busy racin' the day home. Sad folks wake up and say, "Another day." I wake up and say, "There she is again—there it is. Isn't that funny? All this purty stuff doesn't happen 'les I'm there. I get on my knees and pat the earth and say, "God, You done it again! God, You done good. Thank you, feller, friend."

JOHN RUSSELL (HONDO) CROUCH

WINTER'S A WORD TO THE WISE

Protect us, O Lord,
From the cold this winter
That falls below the temperature.
Wearing our coat and hat won't save us.
Snow and ice are not the problem.
Some of us are buried to our ears
In drifts of envy and fear.
The chill factor is
Subtler than the wind.
We shiver from the gust of rage
That blows out the brains
Better than a bullet.
Let this foul weather
Teach us about our true environment.
We go to church not simply to be
Plowed out, but to be thawed.
Let April come this year
To the maples and
To me.

10

The Five Steps

Prayer is God's command performance. He made the first move; so praise such as we have just sampled turned into the traditional first step in formal prayer.

And in their disciplined devotion the saints took praise to mean not only enjoyment as we have seen but also adoration and awe. We don't breeze into the presence of God blowing off steam, disrespecting Him by using Him as a sounding board. If subjects enter the throne room of an earthly king upon their faces, consider the reverence required "where angels fear to tread." If you don't approach the President, or even the "God-father," with a reckless whack on the back, who would dare barge in on Him "Who has you and me, brother, in His hands"?

God pounced on Isaiah, branding him with a hot coal on the mouth. Of course Isaiah was afraid, not that God would hurt him, but afraid for his own unworthiness. The same with the disciples. As soon as Peter perceived that he was standing before Christ, he fell down pleading, "Depart from me for I am a sinful man, O Lord." "Are you afraid?" asked Mole, in *The Wind in the Willows*. Rat replied, "Of him? Oh, no. And yet, O Mole, I am afraid."

So structured prayer begins as we put God carefully into first place, in the highest place. Prayer is not always our little haven of peace and quiet; it is also a restricted zone, an area mined with divine explosives. Prayer is not only our cry, it is holy ground. The psalms often begin with brutal honesty, but never with palaver.

"Be still and know that I am God." Adoration is the vestibule of prayer.

The second step in prayer is thanks. We are not very good at it. We've turned thanks into niceness. Ten lepers were healed. Only one remembered his Saviour. A lifeguard recently reported that he had rescued 223 people from drowning. Three of them thanked him. How many thankful people do you know? We mistakenly equate punctilious "bread and butter" experts with grateful hearts. "Did you say thank you?" We have reduced thanks simply to thank-you notes. We have taken the largest experience a person can have and squeezed it into good manners.

A sweeping statement is not thanks. Thank you—for what? As we have seen, thanks begins to burn in us as we distinguish specifics: the tiny hand that held ours so tightly that uneasy afternoon, the day the barn burned down and for the first time there was nothing between us and the neighbors. Betsie ten Boom, in Ravensbruck, began to count fleas as blessings because they were keeping the Nazi guards out of the women's barracks. Thanks needs no prompting: a good night's sleep, that axe that didn't fall, a burden that is not too heavy.

An army was dying of thirst. Two soldiers risked their lives to find water for the king. The king so appreciated what they had gone through for him that he sensed that their sacrifice had made the water too precious for any man to drink alone. King David poured it out on the ground as an oblation to God.

I know so well what I am owed. Perhaps if I ever knew all I owe, it would pour me into the needle's eye that leads to heaven.

When thanks goes deep enough it comes to confession, prayer's third step. Anyone who sees how right God is soon sees how wrong he himself is. One cannot appreciate God very long before he notices that someone hammered nail holes into His hands. Someone? When one draws near the Light of the World, our hands, our empty hands, are exposed. How dirty are our hands? As we draw nearer and the light grows brighter, do we not find our hands bloodstained? What do we mean when we pray, "We have done those things we ought not to have done," unless we mean at least that?

The curse of the elder brother, who appears many more times in the New Testament than just in the story of the Prodigal Son, is this obnoxious smugness that he was OK. No confession will ever come from him. He can't think of anything to apologize for: "Lo, these many years do I serve thee, neither transgressed I at any time thy commandment..." (Luke 15:29).

But we shall know that we're going home, going straight, when the sins of others shrink to splinters beside our logs. When we too come to the place where, instead of being outraged by the murder others are getting away with, we become, like the prodigal, outraged by ourselves. I am "no more worthy to be called thy son: make me as one of thy hired servants" (Luke 15:19).

When someone can see his own sin, then clearly he is making more than a pass at prayer. He is ready for a giant step.

The hallmark of Christian devotion is caring for the other fellow. We call it intercession. Moses made us an example once. While he was up on the mountain collecting commandments, the people bowed down to a calf of gold. It made Moses mad. But after his fury passed, so did all his pettiness. He made a prayer to end all prayers about being happy in heaven with so many in hell. Moses prayed, "Oh, this people have sinned a great sin, and have made them gods of gold. Yet now, if thou wilt forgive their sin—; and if not, blot me, I pray thee, out of thy book which thou hast written" (Exodus 32:31, 32).

Intercession stretches beyond our front porch to include those "who despitefully use you." "Pray for your enemies," He said. This reminds us that His closing prayer was spent on those who kicked in His face, ground thorns into His skull and crossed Him out. I pray that I'll not only be able to make my prayer like that; I also pray that His prayer, for which He saved His last breaths, includes me too: "Father, forgive them, for they know not what they do." One is never more certain than when he is near that cross, as the late Cardinal John Wright said, "that ninety-nine are not enough for God."

And prayer won't stop there. One final blow to pride remains. You must put in a word for yourself. Even He cried from the cross, "I thirst." So no expert on prayer can get away without crying "help," not only at the beginning, but at the summit of his pilgrimage, after the best that he can do.

Praying for oneself is often condemned as selfish, and only excusable when making the first faltering step toward God. To the contrary, our most adult move may not be thanks or intercession, but the embarrassing conclusion that except for the grace of God, tomorrow we are no better, and no better off, than the neediest wretch of all. It was the Master Himself, immediately after the first communion at the Last Supper, who prayed as any beggar, "Father, if it be possible let this cup pass from me."

When someone says, "God's not interested in little old me," he has just eliminated the pinnacle of prayer. Praying for oneself can be selfish, but it is also humbling, so we pray not simply to the God of Abraham, the God who sees each sparrow fall and counts each hair on every head; each of us prays, as Augustine said, "to Him Who cares for all as He cares for one; and cares for each as He cares for all."

NEVER SAY AMEN

My heart goes out to the one in need
For which there is no federal agency, and
To anyone who is dying
In an inappropriate place
That's not been recognized as
A disaster area.
I feel for someone who's forgotten
What it's like to have kisses blown
To them,
Who can't remember when anyone
Ever cared enough to run to greet them.
I pray for those whom no one
Waits for, or
Stays up for, especially
The one who isn't missed
When he doesn't come.
I weep for those who are beyond
Help and those where help would be
Beneath them.
Teach me how to pray first for the one who
Always comes in last,
For the nobody for whom no one prays—
To catch the names of those
Whose cells and shirts are only
Numbered.
Please God, pray for my lost soul unless and until
I've learned to pray for
My enemies.
O Lord, let me never say
Amen, so long as anyone's left
Who needs a prayer that You've put my legs on.

11

Don't Tell

Christianity is to be shouted from the roof. "No one hides a light under a bushel." "Whosoever confesses me before men, him I will confess also before my Father. . . ." Be seen in church. "Stand up and be counted." "Where's your Bible?" "If these [people] should hold their peace, the stones would immediately cry out."

But we have learned this part too well, particularly when we get credit. There is a paradox here. As soon as our Christianity surfaces, it is tempted to go on stage. Our faith can become a show, a trick we perform for each other instead of our all for God. By going public with our faith we can lose our insides. Perhaps the Lord's Prayer itself suffers from overexposure.

Christianity is not synonymous with being seen in church with a Bible under your arm. Armpit Christians. The true Christian is somehow underground. He is not in uniform. It is a secret service. The members of the true church are known only to God.

Christ called for secrecy first among His disciples. He abhorred a display-window faith. If you become a Christian, don't send out announcements. Don't let on. Don't lay on the horn to blast the way in front of you. Mum's the word. In the sixth chapter of Matthew, Jesus puts Christianity under wraps. Be careful not to make a show of your religion before men. "God will never give you any reward for that," He said.

"Thus, when you do some act of charity, do not announce it with a flourish of trumpets, as the hypocrites do in synagogue and in the streets to win admiration from men. . . . No, when you do some act of charity, do not let your left hand know what your right is doing; your good deed must be secret, and your Father who sees what is done in secret will reward you" (Matthew 6:2–5 NEB).

Lloyd Douglas wrote a novel entitled, *Magnificent Obsession.* The title referred to the hero's lifelong commitment to secret generosity. He represents an endangered species. To be generous is hard enough, but to be anonymous is beyond me. My idea would be to make an anonymous gift that could be traced. Then I would be credited both for the charity and the brave selflessness of not wanting credit. Our tragedy is ever so subtle. We crave the approval of men more than the approval of God.

I know of a huge church that publishes a list in the narthex of members' pledges, with notations of those who are behind. I don't know what that church does with the sixth chapter of Matthew. I am even worse because I don't want my giving to be found out, not because God won't reward me, but because men won't be very impressed either.

Who gives because of God—and not to please or perform for the people? *That* person is very close to the Kingdom. Any gift *that* person makes will be blessed many times over.

In Robert Bolt's play *A Man For All Seasons,* Sir Thomas More tries to get Richard to be a teacher, but Richard wants More to give him a prominent office, so he will be visible. So when More says: "Richard, be a teacher." Richard answers: "Who would know?" And More replies: "God would know and you would know. Quite a public that." That's the public Christ asks us to pray to. We're not to be concerned with what "they" say. But what He will say.

This calls for an unbelievable modesty in Christianity, for our churches are currently patched together by the approval of men. I helped someone move last week. I did it because I was indebted to this person, and I cared for this person. And it did occur to me that this person might think to help me back. No one would question that, but it is not up to this verse "not to be seen of men." Mother Teresa does not help the dying beggar for his applause, or for the Pope's, or for the media's—all those interrupt her passionate belief that when she touches that vermin-ridden derelict, "one of these least," the worst, she is touching the blessed body of Christ. Her reward is not TV. She has no bumper to put a sticker on. God has sent us an angel.

> Again when you pray, do not be like the hypocrites; they love to say their prayers standing up in synagogue and at the street-corners, for everyone to see them. I tell you this: they have their reward already. But when you pray, go into a room by yourself, shut the door, and pray . . . in secret . . . In your prayers do not go babbling on like the heathen, who imagine that the more they say the more likely they are to be heard. Do not imitate them. Your Father knows what your needs are before you ask him.
>
> Matthew 6:5–8 NEB

Often we give the impression that a person has made a huge step forward when he can pray aloud. That may be the death of us. Jesus objects to prayers being broadcast. God not only wants to talk to you alone; Abraham, Moses, and Elijah never heard Him any other way. God holds His peace until He has someone's complete attention. Jesus spoke with God at the Last Supper in front of the twelve and wanted Peter, James, and John to pray with Him in Gethsemane. But it is quite clear by the way He rose a great while before dawn, and the times

He went up into the hills alone, that prayer for Him was not social work but done in isolation. One time it was a self-imposed quarantine that lasted for over a month.

Obviously, not making a show of your religion doesn't mean anything if you don't have any. Modesty means nothing if you have nothing to be modest about. But to believe so deeply in Christ that you pray all night, and to go without eating for days, and to give away a gift—to keep mum about all that, puts you into another category. That is a Christian who means business. That person gets the reward of God.

Time after time Jesus helped someone, then gave him strict instructions to keep it quiet. I've heard scholars argue that He did this because they would otherwise crown Him prematurely, or it would arouse Herod's envy, or draw the attention of the police or His religious competitors, the Pharisees; it never occurs to our vanity that Jesus actually did not want credit and was simply setting the example He wanted us to follow.

Jesus' second temptation in the wilderness overwhelms me. It is such a sneaky temptation. What's so wrong about it (we ask, as it kills us)? "The devil then took him to the Holy City and set him on the parapet of the temple. 'If you are the Son of God,' he said, 'throw yourself down; for Scripture says, "He will put his angels in charge of you, and they will support you in their arms, for fear you should strike your foot against a stone" ' " (Matthew 4:5–7 NEB).

Jesus refused to show off. The temptation to parade our virtues is so easy, and it no doubt is the crime committed by so many "good" Christians. But we're done for if we haven't done something without being paid in reputation. What have I done for God, behind men's backs? Am I any good—without an audience? Have I ever made a hole in one, or caught a big fish for God that I had the strength to hide? That's a Christian! A Christian is not someone who does good deeds and loves his neighbor, but someone who gets away with this without anyone knowing.

No wonder Jesus said, "Beware when all men speak well of you," for then one must have kept busy pleasing them instead of covering one's tracks for God.

In the ninth chapter of Matthew: "Jesus was followed by two blind men, who cried out, 'Son of David, have pity on us!' And when he had gone indoors they came to him. Jesus asked, 'Do you believe that I have the power to do what you want?' 'Yes, sir,' they said. Then he touched their eyes, and said, 'As you have believed, so let it be; and their sight was restored. Jesus said to them sternly, 'See that no one hears about this' " (Matthew 9:27–30 NEB).

"When you do some act of charity, do not let your left hand know what your right is doing; your good deed must be secret, and your Father who sees what is done in secret will reward you" (Matthew 6:3, 4 NEB). This was His "magnificent obsession." It's the way all true Christians are. You know best that you've been prayed for when you don't know who did it.

A LITTLE RELIGION IS WORSE THAN NONE

Heal someone, Father in heaven,
Of some old sore from which he has
Suffered long enough
To prove You are still God
And the trip to church is still worth it.
And while You're up, please fix those of us
Who can't complain, but
Can't sing Hallelujahs either.
That's a bad place to be in,
For there's not much need and not much thanks,
Just enough religion to get by
Without being helped.
There must be some way out
Of a faith that is not
Very interesting or very important.

Deliver us from this vicious circle of
Going around crying out
"I'm fine. How are you?"
So many of us have been stuck in this
Knothole for years, though everyone knows
The joy's not coming out our ears.
Help us to do something
We've never done before—to admit
We're not as saved as we've said we were,
Or we'd be raising the dead by now
And hospitals busy bussing their sick
To our door. Some ministers must be kidding.
There must be millions of Christians
Not quite on the level,
For surely something's delaying

The coming of Your long expected
Kingdom.
Help us to prove
That we were in church today
Better than by pointing to someone else
Who saw us there.

12
Bottoming Out

What about those intrepid saints who give themselves completely to God in ceaseless prayer—where the steps take them not only out of the public eye but to His Cross? Henri J. M. Nouwen, a Catholic priest, has written their book, entitled, *The Way of the Heart* (Seabury Press, 1981). It is about "The Desert Fathers, who lived in the Egyptian Desert during the fourth and fifth centuries; . . . once the persecutions had ceased, it was no longer possible to witness for Christ by following Him as a blood witness." But if the world was no longer the enemy of the Christian, then the Christian had to become the enemy of the dark world. The flight to the desert was next.

I am ashamed to say that I had written off these spiritual extremists as freakish hermits. I had too easily assumed that monks such as Simeon Stylites were simply escape artists. The reader may remember that Simeon lived his life aloft on a pillar performing his devotion in a cyclic pumping motion, which Twain caricatured as only practical if he were harnessed to a sewing machine. Then he would at least have so many shirts a day to show for his otherwise futile marathon.

It is always embarrassing to find some true spirits beneath our broadside ridicule, and the laugh now may be on us whose world has become a noisy chicken coop of confusion—where as T. S. Eliot has written, "The lights must always be on, the music must always play."

Many observers have noticed the alarming comparisons of our world with the decadent Roman world from which the desert fathers fled. According to one spokesman, we Americans who were once independent farmers, then skilled craftsmen, have now become merely clerks, 60 percent of us in information services.

Our library stacks are now so high and growing so fast, no expert can possibly keep up with the proliferation of data in the tiniest field. A new electronic device can concentrate an incredible number of volumes on an area the size of a period, reminiscent of the sterile discussions of yesteryear on how many angels could dance on the head of a pin.

We are so full of questions and answers, and we'll pay schools whatever is necessary for more. This is no longer the age of anxiety, which reflected some wisdom on our predicament; this is the age of advice. Nothing arouses our pity like the poor fellow who hasn't read a newspaper. Our heroes are people who have a lot of information. But our fury of fact-finding and terror of missing something cannot be called creative.

The threat of Communism and nuclear disaster is hardly as appalling as the prospect of having an archaeologist digging in our ruins someday sighing, "These people talked themselves to death." The dreadful way to die may not be on the battlefield but with our television sets playing us. As Malcolm Muggeridge has put it, "I not only disagree with everything they say, I will defend to the death my right not to have to listen to it."

About A.D. 251 when the world was about where we are now, though on a much smaller scale, a boy named Tony was born. At eighteen he heard the words, "go and sell what you own and give the money to the poor . . . then come and follow me" (*see* Matthew 19:21). Not having the protection of Dr. George Buttrick's fine sermon on this text, which suggests that this was not wholesale advice but only an individual prescription to the rich young ruler, Tony took it himself.

Tony left for the Sahara and lived alone and in silence for twenty years. It turned him completely around and into Saint Anthony.

His experience at first was far worse than martyrdom. Then after his version of Jesus' forty days and forty nights, he won such a victory over life that the world beat a path to his door. He became the patron saint of thousands across the centuries. Thousands of churches and hospitals have been named for him. He lived to be 106, and out of his solitude and his silence, he learned to love others like Christ.

Many like to think that Christian conversion takes place at a revival in a crowd, at least in a small group with a fatherly hand upon your shoulder. It can happen that way as it did at Pentecost to three thousand (*see* Acts 2). But the desert fathers testify that that experience is not so likely on the streets and in society; it is a hard-won desert experience: "Solitude is the furnace in which this transformation takes place." Apparently Saint Paul agreed, for his seeming quick-change event en route to Damascus was followed by several years of solitude in Arabia.

Henri Nouwen suggests that today's Christian, even the one who insists on having been born again, is often an unknowing victim of a compulsive religious life. Instead of being forced to face himself, he is propped up by a heavy assignment of "musts" by domineering religious leaders. He makes himself believe Jesus wants him to keep everybody happy, so he never receives Jesus' word as Tony did. He is distracted by too many compulsory meetings, pleasing everyone else. He is swallowed by a schedule of good things that are not good enough. He is never allowed to stop and wait till his anger and frustration come out and his very own light comes on.

In solitude this false scaffolding collapses. Since there are no books, no telephone to run to, no meetings, no entertainment, nobody to show off prayers and memory verses to, one realizes one's nothingness. It breaks one.

Alcoholics Anonymous calls it "bottoming out." Early in this agony of isolation, one fantasizes giving long hostile speeches, or being influential, or irresistible. As one perseveres in solitude, these "monkeys in the banana tree," as Nouwen calls them, give up and go away.

This is death, death to the false self. Unless we are crucified with Christ in this way, we will become ill from being servile to others in the assumption we are being Christian, without ever discovering what a fruitless, spineless one we are.

Until this death takes place, the usual "Christian" sets himself above others. To die to our neighbor is to discover that the trouble with the world is in our own heart. We can no longer wonder whether someone else is good or bad, or think less of them in any way; or before we know it, as Henri Nouwen says:

> ... we fall into the trap of the self-fulfilling prophecy. Those whom we consider lazy ... or obnoxious, we treat as such, forcing them in this way to live up to our own views.
>
> Pay no attention to your neighbor's faults, wondering whether they are good or bad. Do no harm to anyone, do not think anything bad in your heart toward anyone, do not scorn the man who does evil. ... Do not have hostile feelings toward anyone and do not let dislike dominate your heart.
>
> Compassion can never co-exist with judgment because judgment creates the distance, the distinction from being really with the other.

Isn't it strange that we learn to love others best by getting away from everyone but God. First, we must face ourselves in the wilderness. God will be close by.

Bottoming out happens in different kinds of deserts. My esteemed friend Don was a distinguished architect in Texas well on his way to his first million. He began to collect beautiful things: a wife, a little daughter, and an enviable collection of delicate white porcelain.

He also began to drink. One night his wife set out his precious porcelain on her bright linen for special guests, but he had made a few stops on his way home from work and he was no sooner in the door when he went into a drunken rage. He kicked out windows, broke doors, smashed chairs, and obliterated every single piece of his expensive porcelain. When he finished, his home was broken, his little daughter traumatized, and his wife was gone for good.

Don continued his drinking rampage with enough control to keep his job, which of course financed his illness. But he began to suffer blackouts. He could find his way home at night but couldn't remember where he'd been or how he got there. This began to terrify him, but not enough. One beautiful wife after another went down before his insatiable thirst.

Finally he ran out of wives, and he began to end up at night at his father's house. His father had also been a drunk but had recovered in AA. His father knew that the needed rebirth was something God had to accomplish: "They that *wait* for the Lord shall. . . ."

One morning the neighbors called Don's father to get Don off their front porch. Don had done who knows how many terrible things that night; he didn't know where he'd been, but this time he couldn't quite make it home.

Don awakened a day later too terrified to go on. He found he had lost track of time; he had been in a blackout for two weeks! In absolute despair he decided to take his life. He went to the closet and got out his dad's double-barreled shotgun. He sat on the side of the bed to see if he could put the barrels in his mouth and still reach the trigger. He could. He felt the sight at the back of his throat. He got up and loaded two shells.

Something his grandmother used to say when she sent him off to school came back to him: "Do you have on clean underwear?" He smelled so bad he decided on a quick shower first. He leaned the loaded gun against the wall.

While he was in the shower, he heard a knock on the door. Should he answer it? He wrapped a towel around himself and opened the door. There were two men, AA friends of his father: "Can we come in and talk?" When he let them in, God entered too, and Don heard His saving words of hope when the men said, "It doesn't have to be this way." It was then Don gave his heart to God.

That was twelve years ago, and by God's grace he has not had to take another drink. And ever since, others around Don have been giving their hearts to God. That's how you know someone has bottomed out—when his life affects other lives that way.

We will know when our heart of stone has turned to a heart of flesh. Our very being itself will preach the sermon instead of bumper stickers. That is what is shown in this story in *The Way of the Heart* about Father Anthony: "Three fathers used to go and visit blessed Anthony every year and two of them used to discuss their thoughts and the salvation of their souls with him, but the third always remained silent and did not ask him anything. After a long time, Abba Anthony said to him, 'You often come here to see me, but you never ask me anything.' And the other replied, 'It is enough to see you, Father.' "

I'M AFRAID TO ASK

Give me the faith to listen to
You, O Lord.
For Your words may be high;
Give me courage
For Your words may be hard;
And the humility,
For they may be simple.
And give me love, for Your answer
May hurt.
So help me God.

13

The Lord's Prayer

What do you want to know? The hands of children are always up. Teenagers want to know how to drive. Older fingers flip through manuals to win friends and lose weight.

What do you want to know? The disciples of Jesus Christ wanted to know something that disgraces our ignoble questions. Driven by a deeper thirst, they asked, "Lord, teach us to pray."

The answer was a priceless treasure. Soldiers gambled for His robe. They missed His two most precious belongings: a cross and a prayer. The prayer still bears His name. It has been kept sacred by the centuries and polished bright by the lips of millions. It is often committed to memory, but all too seldom learned by heart. It is frequently repeated, rarely obeyed. It is so simple, so short, a child may know it—yet so profound, who can plumb its depths? No one can pray it honestly without being shaken as by fire.

"Our Father."   The first word fractures the hermit's life. This plural prayer is not for an only child, but a brotherhood. It slits boundaries, smashes barriers, splits the walls of exclusiveness, bursts the little whispering circles, and shouts welcome, ringing far and wide. The second word hits still harder. "Are we not all children of one Father?" Others hinted; only Christ had dared to go so far as to claim Him as Sire. What good is an impersonal God? This prayer is a son's confession,

and the rest of the prayer is waste until a man falls to his face, making the prodigal's decision his own: "I will arise and go to my Father."

"Who art in heaven."   This is God's world but not His home. His kingdom has not yet come on earth as it is in heaven. We are not what we ought to be. So we point our spires toward the sky.

"Hallowed be Thy name."   How can a man excuse himself for taking "the name of the Lord in vain" to vent his childish rage—whether he swears in verbs, by slamming the back door, or by nursing a nest of unspoken curses at the bottom of his life? Neither is the Lord a cozy pal. We do not treat Him as a crony or as "my old man." "The omnipotent eternal Father" is no hot-water bottle to ease our aches and pains. We boast His royal blood but confess on helpless knees "we are no longer worthy to be called Thy son." He is uncomfortably near but high above us.

"Thy kingdom come, Thy will be done."   We do not mean it. We don't like authority, nor will we give in easily even if He is the King of heaven. We resent this rule and rage and scream at the way life has to be. Men don't like the parts handed out to them—they would beat God at His business. It is all too obvious that most men over most of the years have prayed earnestly, "Thy kingdom not come, *my* will be done." Christ took things differently. In the garden of Gethsemane He drained the bitter cup without complaint: "Nevertheless, not My will but Thine be done."

"Give us this day our daily bread."   Surely we are old enough to take care of ourselves; but are we? We boast of what we have accumulated, but what do we know or what do we have that is not simply picked up? Does it not belong to Him who put it there? Is it absurd to admit our slim margin of breath and bread? Is there a better bread line than the altar

where men kneel? If we have more than enough, is it not more than our share?

"Forgive us our debts as we forgive our debtors." Some say *trespasses,* others insist on *debts.* Both words are right and the oldest manuscripts used both. In either case, the admission of guilt is a stamp of nobility. "Only men and angels fall." Each of us has done things he shudders to recall. Who can blot out memory or change the past? The Lord made us; to Him we must go. To be forgiven, we must ourselves forgive—but forgiveness costs more, for it assumes the punishment. Sin comes high and he who pardons pays. One who replies to wrong too easily—"It's all right"—rights nothing. The assumption of our sins cost Christ the Cross. But we collect our promised amnesty as we cancel out the wrong done us. We pay not as victims but as partners in crime, and we draw the funds on God.

"Lead us not into temptation, but deliver us from evil." This is puzzling; it is Satan who tempts us, not God. But only God knows our capacity for resistance and can strengthen it. Thus one modern rendering of this petition is: "Grant that we fail not in the time of testing." This world is a forge where souls are hammered out. Trouble tries and tortures us up to our ears. We keep falling into a pit. Who can understand the world or fully bear it? But the hill is not far away; a cross still stands; men are made by clinging to it. People walk in darkness, but they cannot fail to see the enormous stones rolled away or the great light from the Almighty. There is death but there is *transfiguration.* Out of the night comes the miracle of morning.

"For Thine is the kingdom and the power and the glory forever." Nothing was more vivid to Jesus than the reign of God, nothing more definite than the ultimate conquest. Men by squatters' rights contest God's rights. But God is master and this is His world. He has bought it with a heart broken, a Son

crucified. The time has not yet come. There is agony, judgment, a dark impenetrable glass, but belief has broken into our dungeon of suspicion. The sun goes under but not out. There are times when the love of God floods the heart and crowds into trust leaving doubt with barely standing room. Then we know by the bright and shining light of all our seeing that Christ has turned the tide of battle. His suffering can save us from our sins, His Cross has clinched the decisive victory, and His prayer has pledged that final day of glory, when heaven and earth, God and man are reconciled forever.

A FOUL-WEATHER PRAYER

God, how easy it is for me
To tell you how much I love You
Under these friendly skies.
I did not have to drive far
Nor fight my way past the guards
To get to church today.
This prayer did not cost me much.

And while I thank You for this
Comfortable advantage,
Now would be a good time,
While the wind's not blowing
And the flood's not rising
For You to deepen and to
Strengthen me,
So I'll have enough faith that,
Though laws were passed against it,
And people turned their backs on me for it,
I would still have enough left
To come here then as I do now
Unafraid to tell the world that
I believe.

14

The Forgotten Secret

The major business of the Christian is forgiveness. We have been commissioned to forgive not only by the Lord's Prayer but everywhere in the New Testament. In Geoffrey Chaucer's time there was a church position of pardoner. That is what we are: pardoners. It is why Christ came and why we go. "Father, forgive them; for they know not what they do" (Luke 23:34). "That ye may know that the Son of man hath power on earth to forgive sins, (then saith he to the sick of the palsy) Arise, take up thy bed, and go . . ." (Matthew 9:6). "For God sent not his Son into the world to condemn the world; but that the world through him might be saved" (John 3:17). "Whatsoever sins you forgive, they are forgiven" (*see* John 20:23). ". . .'Lord, how often shall my brother sin against me, and I forgive him? As many as seven times?' Jesus said to him, 'I do not say to you seven times, but seventy times seven'" (Matthew 18:21 RSV).

A Christian whose life is not filled with forgiveness is faking it. It is Christ's vocation and our main prayer.

Christians often claim love as Christianity's most redeeming feature, but that is not defined well. The Greeks had three words for love: *Eros, Philia,* and *Agape;* and *Agape,* love for the least, the undeserving, has chiefly to do with forgiveness. Christ's love means forgiving love, a second-mile love; it is what love does when it has been betrayed. The Cross not only signifies that He loved us enough to die for us, the Cross means that He crossed out our treachery.

Forgiveness is not only our major task, it is a matter of life or death. "But if ye forgive not men their trespasses, neither will your Father forgive your trespasses" (Matthew 6:15). If we don't make this prayer, we face a death penalty.

A few years ago my physician informed me that an examination had turned up two polyps in my colon. "I believe them to be malignant and we must make immediate plans to remove them surgically." So very early one morning the nurse gave me my soap and towel and ordered, "Go wash up for surgery." What an awfully lonely place the hospital seemed as I walked down the corridor to the shower.

Imagine my relief as the doctor gradually got through to me upon my emerging from anesthesia that the polyps were safely out and not malignant after all. The second night after the operation I couldn't sleep, so I finally asked the nurse for a sedative. Permission for that was not on my chart, but she found that I could take a pain pill. However, instead of putting me to sleep it took me on a trip.

My mind raced on with a mind of its own, so I helplessly let it go. I am not offering this as valid data in medical research, I am only reporting the trip my mind took me on that night. A question kept coming up in my mind: Where did those two polyps come from? According to the Bible, Christians are supposed to produce peace, gentleness, and self-control. I was producing polyps. Would I have to be hauled into the hospital annually to harvest these things? What sowed them in me?

Suddenly, two men came to my mind; two men I hated. I had told myself long before that I had forgiven them. Of course I had forgiven them. I'm paid to forgive. But as I fantasized sparring with them and hitting them in the nose, I found it delighted me. I hadn't forgiven them at all; I just said I had. I didn't really want to forgive. I wanted to be known as someone who forgives. I hated one of those men more than the other and one polyp was bigger than the other, so I named my two polyps after my two enemies and spent the remainder of that trip and days afterward seeking that grace from God necessary so He could forgive my trespasses as "I forgive those who trespass against me."

No doubt anyone who knows me could have come up with a number of other equally valid names for my polyps. But that postoperative euphoria was a revelation to me: Forgive or perish. To carry any chips on the shoulder is asking for it. To live I must not lie down in front of a truck—or carry any grudges.

Albert Camus bravely confessed, "I always forgot. I never forgave." Perhaps that is more our problem than phrasing it the other way around as we usually do; for we must not forget until we do forgive. We must not lay something to rest until it is resolved. We are so anxious to pronounce ourselves cured, or to insist that our pride is no longer hurt, or else the grievance lashes us so terribly we cannot bear to be conscious of it that we bury it where it will not only not go away but will tunnel underground and erupt in some seemingly unrelated symptom.

A brilliant teenage girl who appeared in my office suffered from nervousness and periodic tremors which she called "fits of the shakes." I promptly suggested referral to a physician. She shook her head. "I have been. Won't you listen to me?" I sat back and waited. She began to confide extremely painful childhood memories. As I remained silent, and she gained confidence, she stiffened in her chair and clutched the arms tightly, her knuckles white. Tears scalded her cheeks. She began to hiss through clenched teeth, her stomach full of antipathy against her father.

He was her mother's mouse meekly turning over each paycheck, abdicating all dignity as man of the house, and nightly descending the cellar stairs to be with his favorite "child"— his beer and stamps. She cursed her father and lived out in the conference room the garnered feelings that had almost buried her.

She kept returning to see me even after the last dregs of her legacy of hate had surfaced. I knew that she had discharged her negative feelings and now possessed insight on her problems, which is to be cured in the clinical sense. Then why was she returning?

At hand was a page about a son who had forgiven his prodigal father, so not knowing what else to do, I asked her if I could read to her about a son who had finally forgiven a father very much like hers. She nodded and I was not to the bottom of the page before she was sobbing her forgiveness as generously as she had her anger before.

I saw her a few months later; the pinched face was gone, and so were the tremors. She was radiant, and her eyes were filled with thanks. Thinking back I realized that her forgiveness had hung on her honestly admitting how angry she was. God's grace had moved in as soon as the anger got out.

And I realized something else. There is a time when praying in one's closet with the door shut won't do it. God was telling this girl to pray to Him through someone else. If our confession has not been heard, or the business of our forgiveness is still unfinished, it may be that the Father is forcing us to go through another. As Augustine said, "Without God we cannot; without us God will not."

Forgiveness is the key to every team effort. Everything takes hard work, practice makes perfect, and we must plan ever so carefully. But time after time I've found that the solution had to do with forgiveness.

Homesick for Ohio and its four seasons, and also hoping that a change would be good particularly for our children, our whole family agreed to accept a call to Liberty Church, to move to Sky Farm along the Scioto River, build a stone house with our own hands, and raise beef cattle.

It seemed so idyllic a plan that I sweetened many a social evening boasting of our ambitions, fully believing that such a prospect was a modest goal for so talented and unified a family as ours: three big teenage boys, my wife, daughter, and me. We had no better sense, nor humility, than to announce it in advance on our Christmas card.

Everyone worked furiously the first few days on what I thought was the toolshed. It turned out to be the music shack. After that burst of energy everything went wrong. I had forgotten all about the mud in Ohio. The summer swam by in a sea of hard work. By August when we had planned to be under roof, we were still mired in the foundation, money running out, winter coming on. Each day the Scripture that exposed me burned deeper into my soul: "This man began to build, and was not able to finish" (Luke 14:30).

The house plans never gave away how enormous the project would prove to be. Then the black week came when someone left the garden hose on to pack the fill dirt behind the longest masonry wall since the Great Wall of China. The hose did settle the fill dirt. The wall fell over. It had not cured sufficiently to take such pressure.

The natives had been restless for some time, but we all became so frustrated and dispirited by the extent of the undertaking and how poorly skilled and inexperienced we were for such an extensive effort, that we were reduced to fighting shamelessly among ourselves. I am grateful to this day that no tapes have surfaced of some of the words to which I descended during those dark dog days.

One of the members of our family is a perfectionist and the rest of us just clods, so the drama of our conflict developed between the two. I don't know who opened fire the day the long wall collapsed, but my perfectionist son was into it with the other two boys so fiercely that they headed toward the opposite corner of the disaster area to lay down their tools and hitchhike back home to Florida. The house building was all a voluntary effort, and they were old enough and free to go.

And as the dreams for our building the house together went up in smoke, I climbed into the argument with the perfectionist too. I had been trained by experts. My mother and father had fought before me and taught me everything I know. My father had been an Applachian athlete with very little academic background—so fought as with a great broadsword, making mammoth strokes that missed. My mother was from upstate New York, the sixth generation in the same house. She had taught in college. She fought as with a rapier, never missing, until by the end of the evening my father stood, drawn, in his doorway, covered with "blood." But he always came through with this strong finish. He would wait for my mother to catch her breath, then he'd sigh, "All right, Mother, forgive me for living," then immediately slam his door.

Finally my son called me a name I could not believe he would call his own father, my being a minister and everything. With my training, I knew exactly what to fire back. I'd get him for that. But for some reason I couldn't speak. Perhaps it was because the other boys were about to leave and the idea of everything going to hell took the heart out of me. I found myself saying instead, "Son, you really know how to hurt a fellow." It was the best thing I ever said.

Everything got quiet and when I looked up I saw my perfectionist son tapping on his wall with a trowel. There were no tears, but I could tell from his face that he was weeping. The other boys saw it too, and we were all suddenly at his side.

Many of us are glib with words. Others of us, like my son, don't say things easily, and when they speak it means something. So we were completely unprepared when he said, "I hope you all will forgive me for treating you like ____" and he used a one-syllable word. We could not believe our ears. He was wearing a red New Holland farm equipment cap. He reached up, took it off, and looked up. "O God, I hope you'll forgive me for treating the ones I love best like _____ " and again he used the one-syllable word. Then we were in each other's arms.

That put us back in business building the house. When visitors come they say, "It must have taken a lot of work to build this house." No, that is not what it took. We did work hard, but what built the house was someone's having the courage to say, "I'm sorry," and others swiftly responding, "It's OK."

For the first time I understood the meaning of the Scripture, "Except the Lord build the house they labour in vain . . ." (Psalms 127:1). One cannot build a house, or keep a son, or hold any home or planet together very long without forgiveness.

Forgiveness, finally, is not simply said. To be truly prayed it must be done, as illustrated in the following true story, which is told in *The Angel of Marye's Heights* by Richard Nunn Lanier (Fredericksburg Press, 1961).

Most of us remember the Battle of Fredericksburg, in the War Between the States, in the poem about Barbara Frietchie, who stopped Stonewall Jackson when he was marching his Confederates through town, by waving the Stars and Stripes in his face: " 'Shoot if you must this old gray head, but spare your country's flag', she said."

However, a far more memorable exploit actually happened there, thanks to the courage and compassion of a young Confederate soldier, the likes of whom we need today as never before.

General Ambrose Burnside's army of the Potomac, about 118,000 men, occupied Fredericksburg by December 12, 1862. Seventy-eight thousand soldiers under Robert E. Lee were streched out for almost six miles along the hills west of town. The strongest Confederate position was on the slopes of Marye's Heights, the lowest hill.

At the foot of Marye's Heights ran the sunken road. Its stone walls afforded the Confederates excellent cover. So when Sumner's Northern troops charged Marye's Heights they were mowed down as though cut with a scythe, by General Cobb's hidden Georgia marksmen. The Federals were taken completely by surprise at point-blank range. French and Haycock's men went down, then Howard's. Finally charges by Sturgis and Getty met the same fate. Griffin's and Humphrey's divisions made the last desperate charges against this impregnable southern fortification behind the natural stone barricades of St. Marye's sunken road.

Northern General Couch shouted: "The whole plain is covered with Yankees, prostrate and falling . . . I have never seen fighting approaching it in uproar and destruction . . . great God, see how our poor fellows are falling. I am losing. Send two rifle batteries."

Upon seeing the almost complete destruction of the Northern offensive in that area Southern General Longstreet said to Lee: "Such bravery is worthy of success." Lee still feared the Federals might break through. But when Longstreet directed that an idle cannon also be trained on that field, his artillery officer replied: "General, we cover that ground now so well that a chicken could not live on that field when we open on it."

The night of the thirteenth the temperature was near zero. All day on December fourteenth the skirmishing was incessant. Between the lines, before the wall, the field was covered with dead and wounded Federals crying for water.

Safely behind the wall Sergeant Richard Kirkland, Company E., 2nd South Carolina volunteers, couldn't bear the cries of the wounded and dying enemy any longer and went to his captain for permission to take them water. The captain told him he would have to get the general's permission. General Kershaw was an old friend of Sergeant Kirkland and his family.

Kirkland approached him, saluting: "General, I can't stand it any longer. I want your permission to go and give those poor men out there some water."

General Kershaw regarded him for a moment with profound admiration then said: "Kirkland, don't you know you would get a bullet through your head the moment you stepped over that wall?" "Yes, sir," he said, "I know that, but if you will let me go, I am willing to try it."

After a pause the general said, "Kirkland I ought not to allow you to run such a risk, but . . . I will not refuse your request. Trusting that God may protect you, you may go." General Kershaw afterwards said: "I felt, when I gave young Kirkland permission to go over the wall, that I was signing his death warrant."

The young sergeant . . . said: "Thank you, sir," and ran down the stairs. The General heard him pause for a moment then return up the stairs to the general's battle headquarters. He thought that Kirkland's heart had failed him. But he was mistaken. The sergeant stopped at the door: "General, can I show a white handkerchief?" The general slowly shook his head. . . . "All right, sir, I'll take the chance."

It was the afternoon of December 14, 1862.

Without further hestitation, Sergeant Dick Kirkland gathered all the canteens he could carry, hastily filled them with water, and without rifle, sidearms, or a white flag, went over the top of the stone wall. General Kershaw watched him sprint to the nearest wounded soldier. A hundred muskets were leveled at him, but not a one was fired.

Was it sheer admiration that held the Federal fire, or the hand of God?

The sergeant knelt down, tenderly lifted the drooping head of a wounded Federal . . . placed the canteen to the parched lips . . . placed his knapsack under his head for a pillow, covered the soldier with his overcoat, replaced his empty canteen with a full one, then turned to another sufferer.

All firing stopped on both sides. The young Confederate was not filching their dead and wounded but nursing those still alive. A mighty cheer rent the air from the Northern side, then from the South. From all over the field the cries now came: "Water, for God's sake, water."

When Kirkland exhausted his supply of water, he went back over the stone wall to refill his canteens. Firing immediately resumed on both sides. But when he reappeared on top of the wall, the firing stopped and the cheering began again.

For an hour and a half he carried water, until he covered the requests from the fallen on that field. Then he returned to his rifle behind the wall. He lost his life later in the war. He was an officer by then, shot through the heart, dying as you might expect thinking of others. "Save yourselves men. Let me be. I'm done for. Tell my dad I died right." But by then he had become known and we still remember him today as "The Angel of Marye's Heights."

Now as never before, with the whole world divided by a curtain of iron, we're all done for without such forgiving and compassionate angels.

A PRAYER THAT CHRIST MAY COME TO YOU

I pray that Christ may come to you early
in the morning as He came to Mary that
morning in the Garden. And I pray that
you find Him in the night when you need
Him as did Nicodemus.

May Christ come to you while you are a
child, for even when the disciples tried
to stop them, Jesus insisted on the children
coming to Him. I pray that Christ may come
to you when you are old, as He came into
old Simeon's arms and made him cry: "Lord,
now let thy servant depart in peace for
mine eyes have seen." May He come to
you in your grief as He did for Mary and
Martha when they lost their brother, and
as He offered to do for the Centurion's
beloved slave when he was at the point of
death.

May Christ come to you in your joy as He
came to the wedding in Cana with the best
wine for everyone—and visit you when you
are sick as He did the little daughter of
Jairus, and for so many who could not walk,
nor stand up straight, nor see, nor hear,
until He came. May the Lord Jesus come in
answer to your questions as He once did for a
lawyer and a rich young ruler. And in your
madness may He stand before you in all His

power as He stood among the graves that day
before Legion.

May Christ come in glory to you upon your dying
day as He did to the thief hanging beside Him
that Good Friday; and though you seldom come
to Him, and though you often make your bed
in hell, like me, may you find Him descending
even there, where the Apostles in their
Creed agreed He went so we would
know there is no place He would not
come for you.

15

The Final Inch

"And [the angel] said, Let me go, for the day breaketh. And [Jacob] said, I will not let thee go, except thou bless me" (Genesis 32:26).

There is a time to say a prayer, then forget it. Prayer can become pathological. We finally must tear the grief-stricken away from the corpse. Or perhaps God's silence shouts "No," and we must accept it as Jesus did in Gethsemane. "Father, if thou be willing, remove this cup from me: nevertheless not my will, but thine, be done" (Luke 22:42). But Jesus, like Jacob, demonstrated persistence so strongly in prayer that He actually told two parables "to the end that men ought always to pray and not to faint" (*see* Luke 18).

It is a strange paradox that the very same God who comes before you call, also appears to stall. When I would tell my father, "I'm coming," and he wanted to accuse me of dragging my feet, he'd sigh, "So's Christmas." There are times when the answers to prayer seem to be taking forever.

Perhaps that was exactly what the disciples were thinking when Jesus came up with these two parables. Earlier they had asked, "Lord, teach us to pray," and He had given them the Lord's Prayer to show them how. Perhaps they had tried and couldn't get it to work, and so He told them these two stories so they wouldn't give up.

In the first story Jesus told about a man who didn't have a

bite in the house one night to feed his company, so he ran next door to get some bread. The lights were all out and the doors locked, but the embarrassed host was so desperate he pounded loudly on the door. And the poor neighbor who had finally gotten the kids their last glass of water, and his wife to stop talking, and the dog to stop barking, finally got up to get the bread, not because he was a good neighbor or wanted to help; but just to get rid of a pest. (*See* Luke 11:5–13.)

So Jesus reminded us that God would do no less. If your boy begged for bread, would you throw a rock at him? The door opens to the one who keeps on knocking.

Jesus' other story was about a widow who went to a hard-hearted judge for help. He helped her so she would stop bothering him. Jesus suggested that if even a heartless Scrooge would help you just to get some peace, how swiftly God will come to those who keep after Him "day and night." (*See* Luke 18:1–8.)

Two powerful examples of how persistent prayer worked are in the Old Testament. A Shunammite woman had given the man of God Elisha a room at her house. Then a child had been born to her, thanks to Elisha's prayers. Suddenly the child complained of a splitting headache, then died. The mother laid the child on Elisha's bed and set out to find Elisha. When she found him he sent his servant, Gehazi, to place the prophet's staff on the child's face.

And Gehazi passed on before them, and laid the staff upon the face of the child; but there was neither voice, nor hearing. Wherefore he went again to meet him, and told him, saying, the child is not awaked. And when Elisha was come into the house, behold, the child was dead, and laid upon his bed. He went in therefore, and shut the door upon them twain, and prayed unto the Lord.

And he went up, and lay upon the child, and put his mouth

upon his mouth, and his eyes upon his eyes, and his hands upon his hands: and he stretched himself upon the child; and the flesh of the child waxed warm. Then he returned, and walked in the house to and fro; and went up, and stretched himself upon him: and the child sneezed seven times, and the child opened his eyes.

And he called Gehazi, and said, Call this Shunammite. So he called her. And when she was come in unto him, he said, Take up thy son. Then she went in, and fell at his feet, and bowed herself to the ground, and took up her son, and went out.

2 Kings 4:31–37

The other example of persistent prayer is Hannah's, the second wife of Elkanah. She had no children. Year after year she journeyed to the temple crying and fasting for a baby.

And she was in bitterness of soul, and prayed unto the Lord, and wept sore. And she vowed a vow, and said, O Lord of hosts, if thou wilt indeed look on the affliction of thine handmaid, and remember me . . . but wilt give unto thine handmaid a man child, then I will give him unto the Lord all the days of his life. . . .

As she continued praying before the Lord . . . only her lips moved, but her voice was not heard: therefore Eli [the priest] thought she had been drunken. . . .

And Hannah answered . . . No, my Lord, I am a woman of a sorrowful spirit: I have drunk neither wine nor strong drink, but have poured out my soul before the Lord.

1 Samuel 1:10–15

God isn't interested in fourth class mail. In these great trials of the human spirit God gets the message that someone really means, not some glib headliner one happens to come up with when he is suddenly called upon to pray in front of everybody. Robert Collyer said that "heaven is determined not to hear what we are not determined heaven shall hear."

Augustine's mother, Monica, conducted a marathon of prayer to bring her son back. I have often thought about her. She prayed the years down. Did her first prayers drive Augustine to hell? A mother's love can have the reverse effect. Maybe she was possessive at first, or proud. The more she prayed the worse he got. Was God saying to her, "Do you mean it? Are you ready for My answer?" Did she finally see herself as the problem? Did her prayers get in the way of God's plans, His timing?

Her prayers became a life of prayer. Finally she knelt at the feet of the old bishop of Madura. Like Eli, he answered for God, "My dear, it is not possible for the son of these tears to perish." It was not so long after that that the prodigal Augustine became the saint, most famous and influential of all the fathers of the church after Saint Paul himself. Augustine would take no creidt for any good he did. His transformation was an answer to persistent prayer.

Why does God make us wait? Perhaps with Monica, and certainly many of us, to show us who is God, until the answer we want is God, not just Santa Claus. The delay is also our education in humility. Much of the blessing is in the waiting; it is in our waiting on God, not His waiting on us.

Sometimes our prayer is not answered because there is some little thing we are to do. Perhaps we are like Naaman, the Syrian general, whose blessing was delayed because of his pride.

> Now Naaman, captain of the host of the king of Syria, was a great man with his master, and honourable, because by him the Lord had given deliverance unto Syria: he was also a mighty man in valour, but he was a leper. And the Syrians had gone out by companies, and had brought away captive

out of the land of Israel a little maid; and she waited on Naaman's wife.

And she said unto her mistress, Would God my lord were with the prophet that is in Samaria! for he would recover him of his leprosy. And one went in, and told his lord saying, Thus and thus said the maid that is of the land of Israel. . . .

So Naaman came with his horses and with his chariot, and stood at the door of the house of Elisha. And Elisha sent a messenger unto him, saying, Go and wash in Jordan seven times, and thy flesh shall come again to thee, and thou shalt be clean. But Naaman was wroth, and went away, and said, Behold, I thought, He will surely come out to me, and stand, and call on the name of the Lord his God, and strike his hand over the place, and recover the leper. Are not Abana and Pharpar, rivers of Damascus, better than all the waters of Israel? may I not wash in them, and be clean? So he turned and went away in a rage.

And his servants came near, and spake unto him, and said, My father, if the prophet had bid thee do some great thing, wouldest thou not have done it? how much rather then, when he saith to thee, Wash, and be clean?

Then went he down and dipped himself seven times in Jordan, according to the saying of the man of God: and his flesh came again like unto the flesh of a little child, and he was clean.

2 Kings 5:1-4, 9-14

And finally, God's deliberateness prevents the wrong prayer from getting anywhere. I thank God for not giving me everything I ask for. I am ashamed of so many of my prayers. Some prayers won't bear repeating. The longer we pray, in the name of Christ, the less we pray unworthily, the more we pray the prayers He's waiting for us to say.

In his memorable book *Prayer*, George Buttrick tells about

Galileo going to visit the tomb of that great Saint Anthony we've already introduced. Galileo planned to pray for money, for his mother, his children, and for fame. But as he neared and finally stood in the shadows of that holy place, the inspiration of Saint Anthony's sacrificial life swept his vanity away, and he found himself finally saying an altogether different prayer from the one which he had intended: "I beg you, Saint Anthony, to plead with Jesus Christ for me that he should enlighten my mind and let me invent something very great to further human knowledge."

I shall not soon forget someone else who said to me so short a time ago that he would like to say a prayer. His pilgrimage had finally brought him to the door of death. I know that he had had his heart set on getting well, on leaving the hospital and going to his sweet home again. What would he say, shaped as he now was by such hard suffering, and such grim news as he'd just been given? For some reason, as I waited for him to get command of himself to speak, I was trembling, for I never before felt so surely in the presence of God Himself. At last his lips shaped the words, "Thanks, thanks for everything; thanks for whatever you have left for me." The wait, the interminable, terrible, awful wait, wrung from him the prayer that brought down upon both our heads the blessing of heaven.

God holds back until we pray with passion, until the yawns are gone, and the sleepy, half-hearted hopes and dreams burn with desire. Prayer is only play until it is finally, glory. The Kingdom is no scheme to get rich quick. "Home is dearer when the journey's long." Heaven itself grows more precious because it is saved for last.

Should some of us pray and never say, "Amen"? According to E. Hermon's story entitled, *The Nun of Lyon,* that may be the answer. She was dancing at her fashionable ball. None was gayer or lovelier. Her marriage to the most eligible man of her set was due within a week. Suddenly in the midst of a minuet, she saw a vision of a world dying—for lack of prayer.

She could almost hear the world's gasping, as a drowning man gasps for air. The dance now seemed macabre, a dance of death. In the corner a priest, smiling and dissatisfied, discussed the eligibles with a matchmaking mother. Even the church did not know that the world was dying—for want of prayer. As instant as a leaping altar flame, she vowed her life to ceaseless prayer—lest the world should die.

Or you and me. A true story came to my attention a short time ago. Two college sophomores were swimming in the ocean. Suddenly he shouted to her, "Swim for shore, sharks!" Something about his voice tore her heart. She swam to him instead. His arm and shoulder had been almost torn off. She brought him in. She saw she could not leave him there. He was dying fast. What should she do? Quickly, she found herself saying, "Are you a Christian?" "No." "Do you want to be?" "Yes." She flew to the water and cupped her hands, then back to his side. And as she poured it on his head she said the final words of that most precious benediction, "In the name of the Father, the Son, and the Holy Ghost, Amen." And he replied, "Oh, thank you," and died.

That girl depicts for me the Nun of Lyon. Could we not join her? Not her order, I mean join our prayers to hers. Help keep an eye on this lonely and treacherous beach. And not only look out for each other, but make sure not to miss anyone who cries: "Nobody gave me a prayer."

> More things are wrought by prayer
> Than this world dreams of. Wherefore, let thy voice
> Rise like a fountain . . . night and day.
> For what are men better than sheep or goats
> That nourish a blind life within the brain,
> If, knowing God, they lift not hands of prayer

Both for themselves and those who call them friends?
For so the whole round earth is every way
Bound by gold chains about the feet of God.

ALFRED, LORD TENNYSON
Idylls of the King

TOGETHER

Father,
The Blessing began
With You.
Grant it may not stop
With us.